First published in Great Britain 2013
Re-printed 2022
A World of Magic Myth and Legend
www. magic-myth-legend.co.uk
copyright Elizabeth Andrews 2013

The moral right of the author has been asserted

FAERIE
FLORA

*Illustrated guide to the folklore surrounding
common flowers and plants*

Written & Illustrated
by

ELIZABETH ANDREWS

Contents

Introduction

Faerie Flora is a collection of traditional faerie lore surrounding some of our most common flowers and plants, showing the close links between the myths, superstitions and the practical uses of these plants.

Even today in this world of practicality and worldliness there are still remnants of the closeness of these beliefs; who has not blown on a dandelion clock and made a wish? Even the cynics amongst us accept the folklore and myths of this country far more readily than the presence of spirits or guardian angels.

The use of herbal remedies has been the only resource available for thousands of years and it still has a lot to offer, although the use of these remedies have to be treated with caution. Some of these plants can be potent and can interact poorly with many medications so it is important to consult a doctor or qualified medical herbalist if you are in any doubt, especially if you are pregnant or breastfeeding.

Spring

The Cuckoo comes in April
Sings a song in May:
Then in June another tune,
And then she flies away

Snowdrop

One of the first flowers of spring, and commonly known as the 'flower of hope'. Although its beauty symbolises purity, it is widely regarded as an omen of death and as such is considered to be unlucky to take into the house of anyone who is sick, except in Shropshire where bunches of the flowers are taken into the house to purify it.

Snowdrop A bulbous perennial found throughout England and Scotland in hedges and woods. Flowers January to March.

Spring Snowflake Rare perennial in the wild but also found in cultivation. Likes the damp woods of Cornwall, East Anglia and Cumbria. Flowers February to April.

Summer Snowflake A rare native bulb found wild only in the south of England. Flowers April to May.

'The Snowdrop in purest white arraie,
First rears her hedde on Candlemas daie'

Circa 1500

Otherwise known as the 'Fair Maid of February', it was customary for young girls dressed in white to walk in procession at the Feast of the Purification.

After Adam and Eve were expelled from the Garden of Eden, Eve stood weeping and surveying the snowy wilderness to which they had been sent when an angel appeared. The glowing figure caught a falling snowflake, breathed on it and then handed it to Eve:

This is an earnest wish, Eve to thee
That sun and summer soon shall be'

The angel vanished and where she had stood the snow had turned into a carpet of snowdrops.

The leaves of the snowdrop contains the alkaloid Galantamine, which was widely used in medieval Europe to ease pain. It was during the 1950's that a Bulgarian pharmacologist noted the locals using it as a headache remedy by rubbing the leaves onto their foreheads.

Galantamine known under the brand name of 'Reminyl' is being used for the treatment of Alzheimers and for neuro muscular ailments such as neuritis and neuralgia.

The bulbs were used by the peasants to treat children suffering from poliomyelitis enabling them to recover from this without any signs of paralysis.

 5

Primrose

The primrose is also known as 'faerie cups' and is a very magical plant. Faeries inhabit the flowers and hide beneath the leaves and they will do their best to protect the plant from harm and will be very displeased if you allow a primrose plant to die in your garden.

A faerie portal can be opened by striking a faerie rock with a posy of primrose flowers. For your own protection you must use the correct number of blooms (which I believe is five) The rock will split and the entrance will be revealed. The faeries dislike being disturbed and will try to pull you through the entrance into their world and never be allowed to return to the land of mortals.

If, however, you have used the right amount of flowers they will be unable to do so and do not forget, if you wish to see the faeries that reside within, remember to eat a primrose flower first and this will make all visible.

There is a strange legend of a beautiful faerie called Berth who had been exiled from faerie land for stealing a gold coin from the Faerie King's treasure room. As punishment for Berth's crime he cast a spell on the entrance to the underground realm and blocked it with the treasure that she had tried to steal. He also set a huge black dog to guard the doorway. Berth was forced to roam in the mortal world until she could find children who had been gifted with a pure soul to help her. Being unable to touch the gold herself Berth hoped that these children would be able to move the Faerie King's treasure and clear the passage so that she could re-enter the faerie realm. So once a year at the full moon, Berth lures a child to the faerie hill using a fragrant bunch of primroses, the scent of which makes them very docile and biddable. A small secret door leads into the hill which only the child can open. Inside, the treasure is covered in a layer of primroses; these have to be carefully removed before anything can be taken from the passage. The child can have whatever it wishes of the priceless treasure but only what he or she can carry.

The flowers have to be replaced on leaving otherwise the guardian of the passage will be angered, and although the treasure is being slowly whittled away by the children, the Faerie King's hoard is immense and it will be many centuries before Berth can return to faerie land.

Primrose A common native perennial, grows in woods hedges and grassy areas. Flowers March to May. The name comes from Prima Rosa first rose. The flowers have a beautiful delicate scent and are one of the prettiest spring flowers.

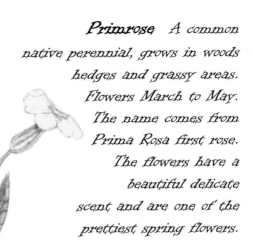

Birds Eye Primrose

A native perennial predominantly found around Yorkshire and Cumbria. Grows in damp grassy areas on peaty soils. Flowers April to June.

Scottish Primrose A native perennial found in the coastal areas of Scotland and the Orkney Islands. Flowers June to August.

The use of the leaves was a well known folk remedy for alleviating arthritis, rheumatism, gout and paralysis (adding leaves to a salad is a good way of doing this) while a salve made from the leaves can be used for soothing wounds, burns and ulcers. Boiling the flowers with elder buds, strained and added to lard was used as an ointment for cuts.

The root dried and powdered is an emetic and an infusion is beneficial for nervous headaches, while a tincture can be used for insomnia.

Primrose Tea

Take 3 tsp of dried primrose flowers and leaves and place in jug, pour over 2 cups of boiling water and leave to steep for 15 minutes. Strain and the tea is ready to drink; it can be sweetened with honey if required. It can be drunk throughout the day; hot or cold and is good for relieving stress headaches and insomnia.

The flowers can also be used to add colour and flavour to custards; can be used to make a lovely pale golden wine.

Primrose Tart

Shortcrust pastry
Sliced apples
Caster sugar
Primrose petals

Line a buttered tin with pastry, cover with layer of sliced apples and sugar, sprinkle with petals and sugar. Cover with pastry then bake.

If a primrose blooms in winter or a single flower is brought indoors this will signal death.

If you have less than 13 flowers in the first spring posy the hens on your land will only hatch 13 chicks.

Bluebell

The bluebell is one of the most potent of faerie flowers and a bluebell wood is a very dangerous place to stray into. It will be full of faeries weaving spells and enchantments amongst the trees in to which you will be drawn if you are not careful.

Mortals will be held captive until led out by another human and if a child wanders into their webs of enchantment they will be whisked away to faerie land and never seen again.

The faeries are called to their revels by the sound of the bluebells chiming but, if a human hears the chiming it means a malicious faerie is nearby and can possibly foretell your own death. For this reason it is known as 'deadman's bells' in Scotland.

If you wish to attract faeries to your home plant bluebells in the garden.

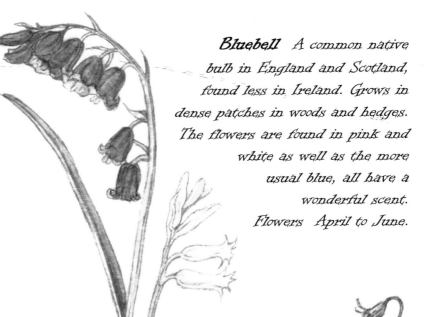

Bluebell A common native
bulb in England and Scotland,
found less in Ireland. Grows in
dense patches in woods and hedges.
The flowers are found in pink and
white as well as the more
usual blue, all have a
wonderful scent.
Flowers April to June.

Scottish Bluebell or Harebell

A common native perennial of Britain,
found on poor dry soils such as banks,
roadsides and dry grassy areas.
Flowers July to September.
The bulbs of the bluebell are poisonous in their fresh
state but have diuretic and styptic properties
and when dried and powdered have been used as
a styptic for Leucorrhoea. Bluebells are currently
being investigated in the treatment of cancer.
The viscid juice contained in the plant has been used
for many things in the past, such as a substitute for
starch, bookbinding gum and also for setting feathers
upon arrows.

13

Cowslip

These flowers are a great favourite
with the faeries and they are
careful to protect the plants from
harm. The smaller faeries use the
flowers as umbrellas and the plants make a good
hiding place when needed.

The plant is known as 'culver's keys' in the west as
they are used for finding faerie
treasure.

Cowslip *A native perennial found in meadows, and on banks in England, Wales and Ireland. Flowers April to May.*

Oxlip

A native perennial, common in a small area around Cambridge. Flowers April to May.

False Oxlip

This is a hybrid between the cowslip and the primrose which occurs when they both grow together. Flowers April to June.

15

The root of the cowslip has similar properties to aspirin and the flowers, which have sedative properties, can be made into a beneficial tea or wine. It also works as an expectorant for coughs and bronchitis, as well as being helpful for arthritis, rheumatism, dizziness, insomnia, constipation and nervous tension.

A compress works well for headaches, and for inflammation; made of crushed flowers and leaves, it is very effective.

Oil of cowslip is good for wrinkles, blemishes and painful swellings and bruises.

Cowslip Tea

Place 1½ oz 40g cowslip flowers into a jug and pour over ½ pt 275 ml of boiling water and leave to steep for 10 minutes. Strain and then drink as needed.

Cowslip Tart

1 pint of cowslip flowers
¼ pint 137 ml cream
1 egg
1 small crumbled macaroon
Pinch of salt
Sugar to taste
A few drops of rosewater
Finely mince the flowers, heat cream gently and pour over beaten eggs.
Stir in other ingredients and pour into individual pastry cases or as a custard in a well buttered dish. Then bake for twenty minutes in a moderate oven.

There was great to do
in heaven one day when
the angels noticed a
small group of people
trying to climb into
heaven by the back
door instead of entering
by the pearly gates.
St Peter heard the
angels lamenting
this lack of reverence
and was so shocked and
upset that he dropped the
keys to heaven.
The keys fell to earth
and took root which grew into
a cowslip plant.

In some parts of the country
cowslips are still called 'the
little keys to heaven.'

17

Tulip

This is a well known tale from the west country about an old woman called Hannah who lived in a cottage deep in the woods. Running alongside the cottage was a small garden where she grew a few vegetables but most of it was given over to a huge bed of the most beautiful scented tulips. These blooms were her pride and joy and she gave them more care and attention than her poor straggling vegetable plants. After a days work in the garden she would sit at the cottage door just admiring the beautiful blooms until the light faded.

One clear still night, Hannah was woken from her sleep by the sound of singing and of babies laughing, she crept out of her bed and nervously peered through the window into the garden but there was nothing to be seen. The sounds were coming from the tulip bed, worried about her lovely plants she threw a shawl about her thin shoulders and hurried out into the garden but as the latch clicked on the cottage door the singing stopped, all was quiet in the garden and nothing could be seen stirring amongst the plants.

By first light Hannah was already out in the garden checking her flowers for damage, but she found they were untouched and there was no sign of anybody ever being there.

The next night was fine and clear and again Hannah was woken by the sound of singing and children laughing. And again she caught no glimpse of her night time visitors. The next morning she went straight to the tulip bed but this time she had taken her glasses with her and she could quite plainly see the little footprints in the soil.

Hannah was delighted to think that she had faeries in the garden and spent the whole day carefully weeding and tending the tulip bed even though her vegetable patch was being overrun by weeds and was desperately in need of watering.

19

That evening Hannah left the front door open so that she could slip out quietly if she heard her little faerie visitors again and then settled down into bed. Her eyelids grew heavier and Hannah could not stay awake for one minute longer.

It was the middle of the night when she awoke, the moon was shining in at the window and she could hear the sound of singing clearly through the open window. She slipped out into the garden and walked down the path to the tulip bed. There in the moonlight Hannah could see scores of tiny faerie mothers standing next to each tulip bloom, gently rocking them backwards and forwards like a cradle while inside lay a little baby.

From then on Hannah tended her tulips carefully everyday and as a thank you the faeries used their magic to make the vegetables thrive and the plants grew so well that soon Hannah had more produce than she knew what to do with.

Then came the day that the little old woman died and her cottage was sold. The family that moved in did not like tulips so they dug up the bulbs and planted parsley in their place. This so enraged the faeries that at night they pulled up all the parsley plants and shredded them. Every plant the new family put in would be pulled up and destroyed until finally nothing would grow in the garden at all.

It was only on Hannah's grave that the tulips still grew big and beautiful, carefully tended by the faeries.

Violet

Violets and pansies are a powerful faerie flower despite their size and are frequently used in faerie love potions.

Avoid picking the flowers in fine weather as the faeries will make it rain in revenge and never pick one with the dew still on it as it will cause the death of a loved one.

The dried leaves and flowers are used to treat bronchitis and catarrh while the fresh flowers can be added to salads and summer wine cups as they are a natural laxative, diuretic and anti rheumatic, while an infusion of the leaves can be used to treat eczema and cystitis.

The violet also has a reputation for an anti- tumour action and their use is being investigated for the treatment of cancers of the breast and alimentary canal.

The green leaves are used with other herbs to make plasters and poultices for inflammations, swellings and piles; fried with egg yolks and applied directly to the afflicted area.

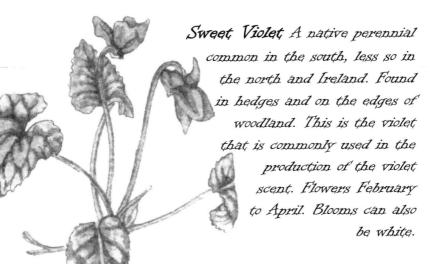

Sweet Violet A native perennial common in the south, less so in the north and Ireland. Found in hedges and on the edges of woodland. This is the violet that is commonly used in the production of the violet scent. Flowers February to April. Blooms can also be white.

Pale Wood Violet A common native perennial found throughout England Grows in woods on calcareous soil. Flowers March to May.

Pansy A common native annual. The name comes from the French word pensee meaning a thought. Flowers April to September.

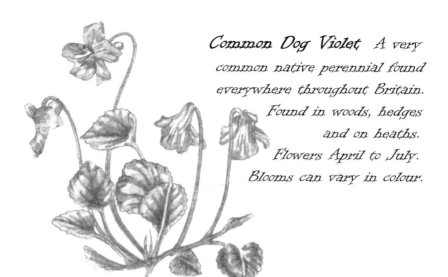

Common Dog Violet A very common native perennial found everywhere throughout Britain. Found in woods, hedges and on heaths. Flowers April to July. Blooms can vary in colour.

Wild Pansy or Heartsease

A native common plant, can be either annual or perennial. Found throughout Britain but rarer in Ireland. This plant is commonly associated with love, thanks to Shakespeare's A Midsummer Night's Dream, where Oberon squeezes the juice of this plant into Titania's eyes so that she will fall in love with Bottom. Flowers April to September.

Mountain Violet or Yellow Pansy

A native perennial found on mountain grassland in central and northern Britain. Flowers May to August. Blooms vary in colour.

24

At the beginning of time when the winters were long and harsh and stretched endlessly throughout the year, the land was ruled by King Frost, from his ice fortress in the north. Each year the snow grew thicker and the people of the land fled before the advancing ice, desperately searching for food and warmth. As the people left, the King became more lonely and remote, his heart grew even colder and so the snow continued to fall. All that stirred around the fortress were the ice wolves padding over the crisp sparkling snow.

In desperation the bravest knights rode to the north to seek an audience with King Frost. Kneeling before the King in his cold throne room they begged him to stop the snow from falling as the people of the land were starving.

These brave men were the first mortals that the King had seen in many years so he listened to their pleas. He told them that if they could find a lovely maiden willing to become his wife, who could gladden and warm his heart, then the snow would recede.

After many months of searching the knights found a beautiful young girl called Violet and took her back to the fortress of icy fortress. The King, on meeting her, fell in love and as the weeks flew by his cold heart melted and he became gentle and kind.

However, after a few months Violet became homesick and she begged her husband to be allowed home to visit her family. Because he loved her so much and wished to make her happy he agreed. So Violet was allowed to return to her home each spring; the King's only condition was that she had to return to her people in the form of a violet, the flower of modesty. Violet was only allowed to stay for the spring and then must return to her husband's fortress.

And that it is said is how the seasons of the year started.

Buttercup

The first buttercup was created by the nymphs of the forest. This beautiful flower was originally a small boy called Ranuculous who dressed himself in yellow and green silk. He spent his days running and playing in the forest, as he played he would sing gaily to himself in a beautiful high pitched voice. The nymphs however found this rather tiring and complained that Ranuculous was disturbing the peace and quiet of their forest. So a great council was held of all the creatures that inhabited the great woods and it was decided that Ranuculous should be banished to the meadows in the form of a flower and so bringing peace and harmony back to their forest, So the boy was turned into the buttercup and he grew and flourished in the meadow, but the forest grew darker and quieter. The nymphs enjoyed the solitude but the other creatures began to miss the bright cheerful little boy and so each day when the sun rose the animals of the forest would venture out into the bright meadow and spend their days with Ranuculous; only returning to the forest at night.

27

Buttercup A common native
perennial, found throughout Britain
in damp meadows. Poisonous.
Flowers April to May.
Rubbing the flowers onto a cows
udders was believed to improve the milk.

Bulbous Buttercup A native perennial
found in England but not so common
in Ireland and Scotland. It is distinguishable
from other buttercups by the bulbous
tubers and the way the sepals bend back.
Flowers April to June.

Creeping Buttercup Perennial of
lawns and mossy areas.
It has long rooting
runners hence its name.
Flowers May to August.

Marsh Marigold or King Cup
A native perennial, found in
wet area, ditches and meadows
Hung upside down in doorways
in May to ward off witches
and to protect from lightening.
Flowers March to July.

28

Foxglove

In China and Japan the fox is believed to be a magical creature and have the power to change shape when needed. Due to this belief in their magical powers they were hunted for their bushy tails which were thought to be a charm against the devil. As the fox numbers fell they begged God for protection against the hunters. So in answer to their pleas he created the foxglove, this he planted in the fields and open spaces, the plant would ring its pink bells at the approach of the hunter and warn the foxes. The faeries also took pity on the fox and picked the little pink flowers (the white markings inside the flowers are the faerie's finger-prints) and placed them over the fox's paws. This would enable the fox to slip away quietly from the hunters. But the wily old fox put it to another use; he found he could creep up quietly on his prey when hunting or even sneak into the hen coups late at night without the hens noticing until it was too late!

Foxglove *A native biennial, common throughout Britain.*

Found in woods, hedges and open areas. The whole plant is poisonous; the drug Digitalis is extracted from the dark green leaves and used in the treatment of heart disease. It was used as a purgative and expectorant which would have been extremely dangerous.

The juice of the foxglove was traditionally used for the treatment of sprains and bruises.

To make cut flowers last longer add foxglove tea to the water in the vase. Pour boiling water over the flowers, or leaves if the flowers aren't in season, and allow to steep for 24 hours. Then add to the water.

The foxglove is a good plant to grow in the garden alongside your other plants as it stimulates growth and resistance to pests and diseases. Another reason to grow this plant is that the faeries adore it and it will be an invitation for the fae to come into your garden. But do not take the flower inside the house as it is unlucky.

Medieval witches used the juice of the foxglove in their spells and it has the power to force the faeries to give back stolen children.

Bindweed

Plant bindweed and morning glory by your gate to keep malicious faeries out of your garden.

The plant was favoured by witches who believed the flower's magic was at its strongest when picked 3 days before the full moon.

Hedge Bindweed

An introduced perennial,
common throughout Britain.
The climbing stems can
reach up to 9ft-3m.
Flowers July to September.

Bindweed

A common native perennial of England,
rarer in other parts of the UK.
Found on waste ground, hedges, grassland etc.
Height to approx 2ft-70cm.
Flowers June to September.

Sea Bindweed

A common native perennial
of British coasts, found on
sand dunes and sea shores.
The trailing stems can reach up
to approx 1½ ft- 50 cm.
Flowers June to August.

Black Bindweed

A common native annual of Britain,
found on waste ground and arable land.
The trailing stems can reach up to
4½ft- 1.2m.
The seeds have a high starch content
and were used as a food source.

Summer

Hall-an-tow
Jolly Rumbelow,
We were up,
Long before the day-o,
To welcome in the Summer,
To welcome in the May-o!
Summer is a comin' in
And the Winter's gone away-o!

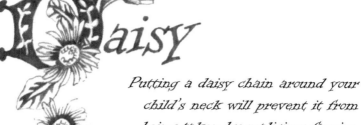

Daisy

Putting a daisy chain around your
child's neck will prevent it from
being taken by malicious faeries.

The belief in the power of the daisy
flower goes back to Celtic times when they believed
that the flowers were the spirits of children who had
died at birth and had returned to earth to comfort
their grieving parents.

Daisy A very common perennial found in grasslands and lawns throughout Britain. The name comes from 'day's eye' as the flower needs a bright day to open. Flowers March to October.

The old name for the daisy was 'bruisewort' as it was used in a decoction mixed with walnut and agrimony to ease the pain of bruises, wounds, ulcers and pustules of the mouth and tongue.

The flower was used in medieval times for the treatment of eye problems and fevers, with this they used magical spells and incantations to make it more effective.

As well as the flowers the leaves can be used, first bruised, then applied to the testicles or any other part of the body that is swollen or hot as this will reduce the heat.

The physicians of Henry VIII used daisies to relieve the pain from his stomach ulcer. The flowers were crushed then steeped in wine and drunk in small quantities. At that time it was believed that the plant could also cure insanity.

Belides was one of a group of dryads who guarded the forests and the meadows. They spent most of their days dancing in the clearings of the forest. This attracted the attention of the lecherous Vertumnus, the deity who guarded the orchards.
To escape his unwelcome advances Belides turned herself into the daisy, 'bellis'.

A fortune telling game for Midsummer Day.

Pick a handful of grass with your eyes closed, the number of daisies that you gather with the grass will indicate the number of years before your marriage, or if you are already wed, the number of children you will have.

Crush a bunch of daisies and mix with almond oil then massage thoroughly through your hair. This will darken your hair and condition it at the same time.

Spring has come when you can place your foot on 12 daisies.

It is good luck if you dream of daisies in the spring or summer, but bad luck if you dream of the flower in the winter.

Daisy chains should always have their ends joined when finished as this represents the sun, earth and the circle of life.

Marigold

The marigold is a powerful aphrodisiac and if
eaten has the power to make you see faeries
and possibly open a portal into faerie land.

It is a well known symbol for good luck and
constancy in love and was used in wedding bouquets
and love potions.

In the west the plant is known as 'drunkards' due
to its reputation for turning people into alcoholics
when the flowers are picked. It has a variety of
names including 'husbandsman's dial', 'marybud',
'marygold' and 'summer bride'.

The Welsh believe that the flower could be used as
a weather omen: if the flowers do not open in the
morning it means rain is on the way.

Hanging a garland of marigolds over your doorway
will stop evil from entering your home as it will strip
a witch of her free will.

Scattering a handful of petals under your pillow will
make your dreams come true.

Marigold This is an annual herb cultivated in gardens but can be found wild. There are many varieties and it can grow up to 18ins- 50cm. The colour of the blooms range from yellow to orange. They appear in early summer and will continue to flower until the first frosts.

Harvest flowers when they are fully open on a warm dry day, dry rapidly in a warm, dark place (airing cupboard is ideal). The colour of the flowers will fade when exposed to sunlight. This is the calendula marigold not the French marigold, 'tagetes'.

The flower of the marigold contains antiseptic properties and the seeds encourage blood clotting, a very useful herb for dealing with the wounded on battlefields. The marigold also contains caretenoids including lutoin which may help the risk of some age related eye problems such as cataracts.

Use dried flowers in an infusion to treat duodenal and gastric ulcers, burns, scalds, cysts and skin lesions, and to promote menstruation.

The juice of the marigold leaves mixed with vinegar eases hot swellings when bathed with the mixture.

The flowers fresh or dried are used in possets, broths or drinks to bring comfort to the heart and spirits; also helps headaches, jaundice, red eyes, toothache, and skin problems.

It has many uses besides medicinal; it is a good companion plant for tomatoes and potatoes and the yellow dye taken from the petals was used for colouring cheese and for hair dye.

The flowers were a traditional pot herb, picked and dried for winter use in soups and stews.

The marigold was valued highly by the Egyptians for its rejuvenation and healing powers and it was also used by the Romans for culinary uses as well as medicinal as they believed it cured just about everything!

For a home made **Marigold Hand Lotion** infuse fresh marigold flowers in an almond or vegetable oil and use as needed. Crushed marigold petals added to an un-perfumed cold cream will cleanse and soften the skin as well as having a soothing effect on sunburn and minor burns.

Marigold Face Pack

1tbsp 15ml fresh marigold petals
1 egg
1 tbsp 15ml oatmeal
1tsp 5ml wheatgerm oil
Crush the petals and pour a little boiling water over them, infuse for 10 minutes. Add beaten egg, oatmeal and wheatgerm oil, then mix well. Apply to face after washing and allow to dry for 15 minutes before rinsing off with tepid water. Pat dry with towel. This will soften and cleanse the skin.

Marigold Tea

Pour 1pt 600ml of boiling water over 1-2tsp 5-10ml of chopped marigold petals and allow to infuse thoroughly before drinking; add honey if required. This makes a soothing drink if you are having trouble sleeping or suffering from nervous tension. It is also beneficial to the heart and eases menstrual pains. Helps with symptoms of the menopause such as hot flushes and mood swings. It can be applied cold to cuts and bruises, and eases tired and swollen feet.
For soothing a wasp or bee sting try rubbing a flower head over the wound.

Rose

Growing roses in your garden will attract the faeries.
If you need their help to cast a love spell, sprinkle rose petals under your feet and dance on them while asking the faeries for their aid in winning the one you love. Hopefully they will give their blessing on your magic.

The rose is the symbol for love, desire, silence and secrecy. In the middle ages a rose was suspended from the ceiling of a council chamber pledging all present to secrecy or 'subrosa' meaning 'under the rose'.

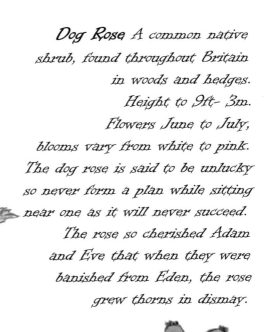

Dog Rose A common native shrub, found throughout Britain in woods and hedges. Height to 9ft- 3m. Flowers June to July, blooms vary from white to pink. The dog rose is said to be unlucky so never form a plan while sitting near one as it will never succeed. The rose so cherished Adam and Eve that when they were banished from Eden, the rose grew thorns in dismay.

Dog Rose Hips The hips were used as a good source of vitamin c for children during World War II. They were encouraged to harvest the hips in the autumn and were paid 3d per lb by the Delrosa company of Wallsend, who then made them into rosehip syrup. Rosehips were found to be effective in the prevention of scurvy.

Field Rose
A common native shrub found in southern and central England and Wales. Smaller than the dog rose, only growing to approx 3ft - 1m. Flowers June to July.

According to Culpepper a decoction made with red roses and wine is a good remedy for headaches, pains in the eyes, ears, throat and gums; it said to strengthen the heart, liver, stomach and retentive faculties.

Rose leaves and mint, heated and applied outwardly to the stomach will help with nausea and vomiting and will help to strengthen a weak stomach.

The fruit of the wild rose made into a conserve with sugar binds the stomach and promotes digestion

Rosehip Syrup

Boil 3 pints 1.7 litres of water
Mince 2 lbs 900 gm of hips and put into water.
Bring to boil then leave to stand for 15 minutes, then strain through muslin. Return residue to pan
and add another 1 ½ pt 852 ml of boiling water, leave to stand for 10 minutes, then strainagain.
Place the juice in a clean saucepan and boil down until reduced to about 1 ½ pt 852 ml then add 1 ¼ lb 860 gm of sugar and boil for further 5 minutes.
Pour into sterile bottles then seal immediately. Store in a dark place.

Rosehip Oil is produced from Rosa Rubiginosa, a rich source of vitamin A (also known as retinol) omega 3 and omega 6 plus essential fatty acids.
It is a light non greasy oil, useful for scar tissue, stretch marks, damaged and dry skin, skin infections, acne, pimples and boils.
It also reduces the size of the pores in facial skin.

Rose Water Wash is a good skin freshener and can be made from either cultivated rose petals or wild rose petals.

Place 3oz 75g fresh petals in a jug and pour over 1 pint, 550ml of boiling water. Wait until it has cooled then strain. Use nightly to freshen skin; it can be adjusted to your skin type by adding a few drops of witch hazel if your skin is oily or a few drops of glycerine if it is dry.

A faerie can make herself invisible by eating a rosehip and spinning anti clockwise on the same spot three times. To become visible again the faerie must eat another rosehip and spin again but this time clockwise 3 times.

 47

Take three roses, white pink and red
Wear them next to your
Heart for three days
Steep them in wine
For three days more
Then give them to your lover
When he drinks, he will
Be yours forever
Traditional love charm.

The rose is under the special protection of King Laurin. He is the Lord of the Rose Garden and rules over the dwarves and elves, residing within a faerie hill which is illuminated by precious stones. The King gains his magical powers from a magic cup, a girdle and a ring.

Four portals to the garden lead,
And when the gates are closed,
No living soul dare touch a Rose,
against his strict command opposed.

In Italy there lies a high mountain range called the Rose Garden; although now barren it was not always the case. In the time of Laurin the slopes were covered in beautiful fragrant red roses and the Dwarf King and his people lived deep inside the hollow mountain, surrounded by glorious treasures. The boundary of his magical kingdom was marked by a thin thread of red silk.

According to legend, Laurin fell in love with the beautiful Similde, a Princess from a neighbouring kingdom. Desiring the young girl for his wife he sent three of his wisest and most courteous dwarves to ask for her hand in marriage. The dwarves set out on the long journey over the mountains and finally reached the castle after many grueling weeks of travel. Approaching the vast gateway they were met by the King's steward, a mean spirited man called Wittage, who sneered at the three dwarves and was reluctant to let them enter the castle. After much persuasion they were eventually led into the King's presence. They knelt before the throne while delivering Laurin's offer for the Princess' hand. The King was horrified that a dwarf was asking for his beloved daughter in marriage and would have had them thrown out there and then, but the three dwarves insisted on seeing Similde to deliver Laurin's proposal in person. Not wanting to anger the formidable Dwarf King he reluctantly sent for his daughter to see if she would accept Laurin as a husband. Similde, was as equally horrified as her father and curtly refused. Wittage's sneers and taunts followed the dwarves as they left the castle bearing the rejected proposal back to their King who

was waiting impatiently on the side of the Rose
Garden mountains.

Laurin was furious with the Princess's response
and being a rather stubborn dwarf refused to
accept Similde's answer, so he strapped on his
magic belt that gave him the strength of twelve
men and set off across the mountains to the castle.
The dwarf crept across the drawbridge and into the
darkened throne room, from there he searched
through all the rooms until he found the Princess's
bedchamber. The Dwarf King snatched up the
sleeping girl and carried her back to his kingdom
inside the mountain where he kept her captive
for seven years.

Then quite by chance rumours reached Similde's
brother of her whereabouts. He already knew of
Laurin's fearsome reputation so enlisted the aid of
Dietrich, a fiercesome warrior from Bern.

So the Prince, Dietrich and his soldiers set off into
the mountains to look for Laurin's kingdom. After
many days of wandering lost in the hills they saw
the rose covered mountain rising above the valley in
the distance and realised that at last they had found
the Dwarf King's enchanted kingdom.

They ventured further into the beautiful scented
valley and reached the silk thread which enclosed
the magical land.

Dietrich diplomatically proposed that they send a
messenger to King Laurin to treat with him before
breaking the silk thread but Wittage sprang down
from his horse, tore the thread and trampled the
roses underfoot. The little Dwarf King immediately
appeared from the hillside, brandishing his spear at
Wittage and demanding to know the reason for this
outrage.

Wittage laughed in scorn at the dwarf and drew his sword. He and Laurin began to fight and it was not long before Wittage was beaten back. In fear of his life he called for Dietrich's help.

The warrior strode forward drawing his own sword from its scabbard but before he reached the fighting men one of his soldiers warned him of Laurin's magical belt. Seizing his chance while Laurin was occupied with Wittage he tore the belt from around the dwarf's waist and held it aloft. With his power gone the little King was soon vanquished by the powerful warrior.

The Prince rode up to the fallen Laurin and demanded to know the whereabouts of the Princess. Laurin answered that Similde was within the mountain and that no harm had come to her over the period of her captivity.

The bruised and bloody Wittage refused to believe him and demanded that she be brought out or he would cut off the King's head.

As he spoke, a small door appeared in the rocks and Similde surrounded by courtiers from Laurin's palace stepped out. The Princess was delighted to see her brother and greeted him fondly with a kiss on either cheek. She thanked him and the brave Dietrich for her release, but told them that Laurin, being a noble King, had treated her well. The Princess did not wish for any harm to come to him and hoped that they could all be friends.

The Prince was relieved and delighted to see his sister well and happy and so offered his hand in friendship to the Dwarf King. Dietrich and his soldiers all followed suit except for Wittage; who refused to make peace with Laurin and slunk off

back down the mountain.

Appeased, Laurin invited his new friends inside the mountain and led them deep into his kingdom, past caverns filled with treasures and beautiful works of art, into the centre of the mountain range to a large hall with tall marble pillars supporting a crystal roof. Laurin entertained his guests to a lavish banquet that lasted well into the night, and when his guest's heads were drooping with weariness he took them to sumptuous apartments that had been prepared.

Later that night Laurin was awoken by one of his shield bearers with the news that Wittage had returned to the mountain with a troop of soldiers and was trying to break in the front gate. The King threw back the bedclothes in a fury thinking he had been deceived by his guests.

He gathered his men and marched outside to confront Wittage and his troop of soldiers. After a furious battle the King and his dwarves drove Wittage and his men, bruised and bloody, back down the mountain. While inside, the Prince and Dietrich had been awoken by the sounds of the battle raging on the hillside. Thinking they too had been betrayed and fearing for their lives they drew their swords and rushed towards the entrance. Just at that moment the dwarves re-entered the mountain and seeing Dietrich and his armed men running down the passageway towards them attacked the men savagely. On the orders of the King the dwarves put on their magical caps which made them invisible to Dietrich and his men.

With this advantage they soon overpowered the Prince and his men and took them captive, the

chained prisoners were hustled off to the keep and locked in one of their strongest dungeons.

Dietrich became so angry at being imprisoned that fire came from his mouth and melted the chains that bound him. Once free he melted with his fiery breath the chains binding his companions.

Dietrich and the Prince had just turned their attention to breaking through the iron studded door when Similde appeared outside and unlocked it. Anxious for the her brother's safety she presented each of the men with a magic ring which would counteract the magical caps of the dwarves. She quickly led them to the nearest door out onto the mountainside but they were spotted and the alarm was raised. A troop of dwarves, wearing their magical caps, rushed to the keep to capture the escaping prisoners. With the magic rings the Prince and his men could see the dwarves this time so they were soon at a disadvantage. The fighting spilled out onto the mountainside and the screams, shouts and clashing of the swords woke the giants who lived farther down the valley. They lumbered up the hillside to aid the dwarves but even with their great size they could not defeat the powerful warrior Dietrich.

Soon all the dwarves were beaten back into the mountain, the giants driven off and the King taken prisoner. He was dragged away bound in chains and kept captive in a small farmhouse with Wittage as his guard. Laurin was held prisoner for many years, often bound to a pillar, frequently tormented by the mocking Wittage.

On one of the many long winter nights of Laurin's captivity, Wittage and his guards became engrossed

in a game of dice. The night was cold and they huddled around a glowing brazier to keep warm. As the night wore on they became more fuddled with the beer and heat until one by one they fell asleep. Laurin watched patientlyfrom the pillar where he was bound until they were all asleep, then dragged himself forward to the burning coals and burnt off the ropes that held him.

Once free he fled from the farm and started back towards his mountain.

Laurin entered the valley and he could see the red roses on the slopes of the mountain ahead, rising above the forest, and realised at once that the roses had given away his secret kingdom. For if Dietrich and his men had not seen the roses they would never have discovered the mountain.

So Laurin placed a spell on the Rose Garden mountain making it barren where no rose would grow or bloom again by night or day, but in his rush he forgot about the twilight which is neither; so the enchanted garden makes a brief appearance at every twilight making the mountain glow with the red roses and wafting their beautiful fragrance out into the evening air.

Nettle

In medieval Europe patients were flogged with nettles in an effort to cure arthritis and paralysis; this practice is still used today by some to cure their arthritis.

Stinging Nettle

A very common native perennial found throughout Britain.
Flowers May to Sept.

The juice of the leaves or roots made into a decoction is good for washing sores, gangrene, scabies, mange, itch, gout and arthritis.
Fresh wounds can be treated by washing with the juice or by applying bruised green leaves.
The leaves once dried can be used to staunch the flow of blood from a wound and it has anti-histamine and anti-asthmatic properties. The dried leaves in an infusion can be used to treat nervous eczema.
For cold and numbed fingers and toes, an ointment rubbed in, made of the juice mixed with oil and a little wax will help restore the circulation and warm up the hands and feet.

Nettle Tea for adults, pour 2/3 cup of boiling water over 3 to 4 tsp of dried leaves or dried root, (fresh leaves can be used) and steep for 3 to 5 minutes.

Drink 3 to 4 cups daily.

Blends well with lemon balm, also honey can be added if required.

Nettle tea is an ideal drink during the menstrual cycle especially if bleeding is heavy, will help with bloating and breast tenderness. Use with caution as nettles can alter the menstrual cycle and it is not advisable for pregnant women to drink nettle tea.

Nettle Tea for Anaemia

½ cup nettle leaves dried
½ cup yarrow leaves dried
½ cup peppermint leaves dried
1 cup of boiling water
Pour water of 1 to 2 teaspoons of mixture, infuse for 10 minutes. Drink one cup after eating.

Nettle Tea to purify Blood

½ cup nettle leaves dried
½ cup dandelion leaves dried
½ cup birch leaves dried
½ cup rose hips dried
1 cup of boiling water
Pour the cup of boiling water over 1 to 2 tsp of mixture then steep for 10 minutes, strain, then drink one cup twice a day. This tea will flush out your system and remove impurities from the body.

The young shoots of the nettle are useful as a food in soups and stews, they are an excellent source of calcium, magnesium, iron and numerous trace elements as well as containing many vitamins.

Nettle Soup

1 lb 425g potatoes
½ lb 215g young nettle shoots
2oz 50g butter
1 ½ pt 852ml vegetable stock
Salt and pepper
4 tbsps 60ml cream
Cook potatoes for 10 minutes, drain.
Wash and chop leaves.
Melt butter into saucepan, add
nettles and simmer for a few minutes, add potatoes and stock. Bring to boil and simmer for 10 minutes or until tender. When cooked puree together, then add seasoning and cream.

Nettle Beer

1lb 425g fresh nettle stalks with leaves
2 ½ gallons 12 ltr water
3lb 1 ½ kg sugar
2oz 50g cream of tartar
½ oz 15g yeast (brewers yeast)
Wash nettles and boil in water for 15 minutes, strain, add sugar and cream of tartar to liquid.
Heat and simmer until dissolved, wait until tepid then add yeast and stir.
Cover with muslin and stand for two to three days.
Remove scum and decant into bottles without disturbing the sediment then cork and secure firmly.

60

If you are unfortunate enough to be stung by a nettle the natural remedy is to find a dock leaf, spit on it and rub the affected part with the dock. The leaf contains a chemical that neutralises the sting and also cools the skin. Do not forget to chant 'in dock, out, nettle.'

For centuries cloth has been woven from the fibres of the mature stem. The juice of the stems and leaves has been used to produce a green dye and a yellow dye can be made by boiling the roots.
The leaves and shoots were collected in vast quantities during the second world war for dying camouflage nets.

The nettle is also a very important plant for wildlife and can support over 40 species of insects such as the small Tortoiseshell and Peacock butterfly larvae.

It was believed many years ago that eating nettles would dispel a curse.

There was once a King who had six sons and one daughter but no Queen and although he loved his children dearly he felt the need for a wife. So he set forth to a neighbouring kingdom and in due course returned home with a beautiful bride. The new Queen declared her affection for the King's children, but in her heart she felt nothing but hatred for his handsome sons and beautiful daughter, feeling that any child she bore would suffer in comparison.

So the evil stepmother waited until the King was busy with affairs of state then told her loyal servant to take the sons out hunting in the vast forest of the King's land.

'Take them deep into the forest and when they are weary and thirsty give them this to drink,' she instructed and handed him a flask of wine into which she had mixed a magical potion. 'Then hurry back and tell me what happened.'

The servant did as he was bid, and as the brothers shared the flask while resting in a clearing deep in the trees they started to change. Their arms sprouted feathers, their necks lengthened and their noses grew into bright orange beaks, until in place of the young men were six pure white swans.

The servant staggered back in amazement as the swans launched into the air with mournful honks, leaving nothing but a single feather floating down on the breeze. He picked it up and hurried back to the palace to show the Queen.

'Excellent! Now no word of this must reach the King,' she warned him.

The King was desolate when he heard that his six sons had disappeared; he ordered out the troops to

search the surrounding lands for them. Each day the weary soldiers returned without news of the missing princes. Days, weeks then months followed and still no news came of their whereabouts. The Queen feigned sorrow while she comforted the King but gloated in private, she then began to plan the disappearance of his daughter.

'You must take the Princess to the forest to pick berries and then kill her. You can say a wild animal attacked her,' she ordered her servant.

The next morning he led the girl deep into the trees to the same clearing.

'Here Princess, rest for a minute,' he gestured to a fallen log.

She glanced around at the bare bushes. 'Where are the berries?'

'We'll find some presently,' he replied, stealthily drawing a dagger from his sleeve but before he could strike, a swan swept down and beat him to the ground with his strong wings. With a loud honking five more swans flew down to the clearing and surrounded the Queen's servant. Their long necks stretched towards him as they hissed menacingly.

The Princess drew back as one bird approached her.

'Do not worry sister, do you not know us? We are your brothers.'

'Oh brothers,' she said in amazement, leaping to her feet. 'What has happened to you?'

'It was the Queen, our stepmother, she ordered this loathsome creature to give us a magic potion and now she plans to kill you.'

'Oh the evil creature! What shall I do?'

'You must come with us, we will carry you to another land where you will be safe.'

 64

The Princess climbed onto her eldest brother's back
and they lifted out of the clearing into the wide blue
sky above. She peered down from the swan's back
and saw the servant running along the narrow path
to the palace.

'He will tell the Queen what has happened.'

'Then we must hurry and fly far away where she
cannot harm us.'

The six swans carried their sister far across the sea
heading for the distant shore and reached land just
as the sun was setting. The princess curled up in
the warm sand and fell asleep while her brothers
formed a circle and sheltered her with their wings.

'Sleep now sister,' they whispered. 'And tomorrow
we will find a new home where we can live in safety
together.'

Come sunrise they flew farther inland until they saw
a small cottage in a valley; the six swans swooped
down and landed gently on the smooth green turf in
front of the door. It was open, it looked as though it
had been deserted for some time.

'This looks just perfect for us,' she declared.

They lived there in peace for several weeks. Each
morning the brothers would fly off to search for food;
fish from the rivers and berries from the hedges
leaving their sister to wander alone in the woods.

The Princess never saw another soul in all her
wanderings until one day she met an old woman
sheltering under a tree.

'Oh,' she exclaimed 'You startled me, old crone.'

'Do not be concerned Princess, I mean you no harm.'

'How do you know who I am?' she asked in surprise
and not a little alarmed.

'I know of you and your brothers plight and wish to
help.'

'You can help my brothers? Can you break my stepmother's wicked spell?'

'Yes, but it is your strength that will be the most important thing if you wish to help them.'

'I will do anything I can,' she said earnestly.

'You have one year to this day to weave shirts for your six brothers and stitch them together with this magic thread.' In her hand she held a golden spool. 'You must collect nettles from the woods, crush the stems and use the fibres to make cloth. But,' the old woman warned. 'You must not speak a word to anybody until the year is up and the shirts finished or your brothers will remain as swans for the rest of their lives.'

'I understand old woman,' as she replied, the old crone vanished leaving the spool of thread lying in the grass.

Her brothers returned at sunset and found her hard at work beating the nettles to a pulp; her hands were red and swollen from the stings but she would not stop no matter how hard they begged. The princess could not explain to them what she was doing, she just shook her head at her brothers and continued working.

Over the months the pile of woven cloth grew bigger until she finally had enough to start making the shirts. The Princess pulled out the spool of magic thread and began to stitch. The first shirt was completed and she had just laid it down on the table when a hunting horn blared from behind the cottage. She leapt to her feet and peered out of the door, hounds ran past the front of the cottage followed by a group of men on horses. One gaily dressed man pulled up at the sight of the beautiful girl standing

in the doorway.

'Greetings. I did not realise there was anybody living in this old cottage.'

But the Princess could not reply and just shook her head at him.

'Come young woman who are you? Answer please,' he said impatiently as she remained dumb. 'Do you live here alone? Where is your family?'

The Prince, because of course he was a Prince, gazed in frustration at the beautiful girl as she refused to speak.

'You must come with me back to the palace where I will look after you.'

The Princess did not wish to go and cowered back from him, but he took her arm and led her to the horse. 'Return with me and I will give you fine clothes and jewels, anything you could wish for.'

The Prince put the reluctant girl upon his saddle and leapt up behind her, but she pointed to the bundle of sewing and gestured that she wished for it so one of the servants wrapped it up and placed it in the pannier on his horse.

The Prince gave her a bedchamber hung with brightly coloured tapestries overlooking the courtyard; she was bathed in rose water and dressed in silks but she still would not speak. Every spare moment she continued to make the nettle shirts, for she was very aware that time was running out. The Prince and his servant tried to stop her as her hands grew so sore. In frustration the Prince threatened to burn the bundle of shirts but she became so upset that he relented. However the servants started to whisper that she was an evil enchantress weaving spells. These rumours eventually reached the ears of

the King and Queen who ordered that the girl should be brought before them. She stood before the court but could not defend herself against the accusations of witchcraft however much the Prince pleaded with her to speak. The Princess just shook her head and remained dumb. The King frowned at the beautiful girl dressed in silks, with her hands all swollen and bleeding.

'She must be a witch, she will not deny it. A pyre will be built in the courtyard and tomorrow the witch must be burnt.'

The grief stricken girl was led back to her room and the door slammed and locked behind her. She had one day left to finish the shirts so threw the rest of the cloth on the floor and feverishly began to cut out all the pieces of the remaining shirts. As the morning sun rose over the courtyard she had reached the last one.

The guards led her out into the courtyard, the five finished shirts were tucked under one arm while she frantically stitched the remaining shirt.

'Oh look at the enchantress still weaving her spells,'' wailed the courtiers as guards dragged her forward to the pile of brushwood.

'Tie her to the post,' ordered the King. A servant hurried forward with a blazing torch. 'Burn her quickly before she places an evil spell on us all.'

The pyre was lit and the flames began licking at her legs and she gazed in despair at the sky. Just then over the battlements six swans appeared. They swooped down into the courtyard and beat out the flames with their wings and pulled off the ropes. As each swan flew past the Princess she threw a shirt over their back. One by one the swans landed

and before the amazed court, they changed back into their human forms.

'Brothers,' she exclaimed, at last able to speak.

The eldest brother helped her from the still smoldering fire.

'We have searched for you far and wide, thank goodness we found you in time.' He turned to the King and Queen who were watching in astonishment. 'How dare you treat my sister so, she has done no harm to you.'

The Prince came forward. 'I love her dearly but I did not understand why she remained silent.'

'I had to remain so otherwise my brothers would not be set free from this evil spell.'

The Prince knelt before the Princess. 'Please forgive us,' he begged. 'Stay here with me and I will make you my wife.'

One of her brothers angrily stepped forward. 'You are not worthy of our sister, after all that she has suffered for us.'

'Do not be angry with him, he could not have known the reason for my silence but now I wish to return home to my father.'

So the six brothers took their sister and traveled home to their father's land. He spied them on the road leading to the Palace and rushed out to meet them overcome with joy.

When the Queen saw the brothers with their sister standing in the throne room she wailed and fled. But she did not escape, she was dragged back by the King's soldiers and hauled in front of the court where she was condemned to the cruel and horrible fate of being rolled down a hill in a burning tar barrel.

Lavender

It has been used for hundreds of years in many ways, medicinally as well as in the use of love spells and rituals. By carrying lavender flowers you can attract spirits as well as bringing peace, love and good health, but it will also give protection against the evil eye. It was traditional to pin lavender to the clothes of young children for this reason.

Where there is lavender there will be a lot of faerie activity, so if you wish the fae visit your garden, plant lavender in your borders, the faeries will bring healing and protection to your house. Lavender mixed with mugwort, rose petals and chamomile at midsummer will attract the inhabitants of faerie land.

Lavender is also prized by witches as it increases their powers of clairvoyance.

It can be combined with St Johns Wort, to be used around mid-summers day.

Wear it to attract a honourable suitor; it will protect your chastity and repel dishonourable men. Brides wear it in their hair as it helps them to retain their female power and bring them luck. And once married lavender bags should be placed under the mattress to ensure marital bliss.

Lavender is a tough plant, and will tolerate most growing conditions but thrives in warm, well drained soil and in full sun. A poor soil will encourage a higher concentration of oils. The flowers appear during the summer and range from purple through to mauve and pin., There are many different varieties and all make excellent companion plants.

Lavender Oil

2/3 pt 400 ml of almond oil or green olive oil
Large handful of crushed lavender flowers
1 tbsp 15 ml white wine vinegar
Insert all ingredients into a screw top jar and shake well. Stand the jar in a sunny place for approximately 2 weeks remembering to shake every day.

At the end of the 2 weeks test the oil by rubbing onto the skin, if the perfume lasts more than a few minutes the oil is ready, if not leave for a further week before testing again.

Lavender oil is good for many skin conditions and is used in the treatment of acne, usually in conjunction with bergamot.

The lavender is a powerful antiseptic and inhibits the bacteria which cause skin infection, at the same time soothing the skin and reducing scarring. It is also ideal for treating burns and scalds as it promotes rapid healing.

For an effective remedy for coughs, colds, catarrh and sinusitis add a few drops of oil to hot water, inhale for 15 minutes. This will help soothe and decongest.

For painful catarrh and sinusitis massage several drops onto the eyebrow ridge, either side of the nose and along the cheekbones. Massage for several minutes in a circular motion, the warmth from your hands will also help ease the pain.

A few drops of the oil added to your bath water will help to ease rheumatism, sciatica, arthritis and muscular pain and reduce inflammation.

If you are unlucky enough to suffer from menstrual pain, gently massage the oil onto your stomach or make a hot compress and place it on your stomach.

Lavender Tea is good for soothing and calming nerves and helps to relieve headaches.

Add 1 tbsp 15ml of crushed lavender flowers to a cup of boiling water and allow to steep for 5 minutes before straining and drinking. This is an effective sedative and will aid sleep if taken at night.

The tea can be used as a cure for colic and dyspepsia, especially if these conditions are caused by depression as lavender is an anti-depressant.

Once cooled the tea can be used as a cold compress to the temples and forehead in cases of headaches.

On St Luke's Day young girls would drink lavender tea and say

> 'St Luke, St Luke, be kind to me,
> In my dreams, let me my true love see'

Lavender Wash

This wash can be used twice a day for skin problems and is also helpful in the treatment of spots.

Place 4 oz 125g of fresh lavender flowers into a bowl and pour over 1 pint 600 ml of boiling water and leave to cool. Strain and then apply when required.

Another remedy for acne is **Lavender Vinegar**

Place 1 cup of fresh flowers into a screw topped jar or bottle and pour in enough white vinegar to cover, then leave in a cool dark place for 1 week. Remember to shake once a day then strain and keep in a clean jar ready for use.

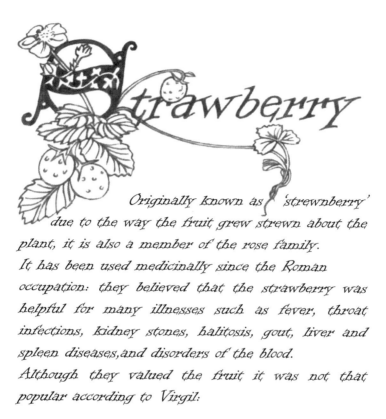

Strawberry

Originally known as 'strewnberry' due to the way the fruit grew strewn about the plant, it is also a member of the rose family.

It has been used medicinally since the Roman occupation: they believed that the strawberry was helpful for many illnesses such as fever, throat infections, kidney stones, halitosis, gout, liver and spleen diseases, and disorders of the blood.

Although they valued the fruit it was not that popular according to Virgil:

> 'Ye boys that gather
> Flowers and Strawberries
> Lo, hid within the grass
> An adder lies.'

The belief that the fruit was contaminated by adders and toads continued up until the 12th century.

The cultivation of the strawberry began around the 1500's but it was not until the 1700's with the cross breeding of varieties from America and Chile that the bigger fruited strawberries began to appear.

> 'Doubtless God could have made a better berry,
> But doubtless God never did'
> Dr. William Butler

Wild Strawberry *A common native perennial. Found in dry hedges, grasslands and woods. The wild fruit has a stronger flavour than the cultivated fruit. Flowers April to July and fruits June to August*

Strawberry leaves used in a poultice will help in cases of acne. Apply the wetted leaves to the face to improve the complexion. A cut strawberry rubbed over the face after washing will also help clear the complexion and whiten the skin.

Wild Strawberry

An infusion of leaves or roots of 1 oz 25 g to 1 pt 600 ml boiling water is a useful mild astringent and diuretic. Good for urinary disorders and it has a mild laxative effect.

Strawberry Sunburn Remedy

Take a ½ lb 250g of really ripe fruit and mash thoroughly then mix with ½ pot of plain yogurt. Spread this over the sunburned skin and it will cool and soothe it.

Strawberries are high in boron which helps raise the levels of estrogens so are good for menopausal women.

The fruit is rich in vitamin C and contains potassium, folic acid, and vitamin B6. It is also high in fibre and is good for helping to reduce cholesterol levels, and as well as all that, it was believed to be an aphrodisiac!

Young couples were given strawberries on their wedding night and if you found a double fruit by splitting it and giving it to a member of the opposite sex they would become your true love.

In Europe the fruit is sacred to the Virgin Mary. She walks with the children as they go strawberry picking on St John's Day, so any mother that has been unlucky enough to lose a child will not pick the fruit on that day in case her child misses out in paradise.

Every spring in Bavaria the local farming families would tie little baskets of wild strawberries to the horns of their cattle as an offering to the elves of the woods. In return the farmers hoped the elves would wish them well and help look after the cattle, ensuring plenty of healthy calves and milk.

Tiny seeds of the strawberry were discovered at Mesolithic sites in Denmark, Neolithic sites in Switzerland and iron age sites in England.

Strawberries in Winter

This is a traditional Slovakian folktale, very similar to our Cinderella faerie tale.

Ella lived with her stepmother and stepsister in a large house at the edge of the forest. Her father had died the previous winter from a fever leaving her alone. Although Ella was not as pretty as her stepsister she was kind and good and was a great favourite with all the visitors to the house. Her father had been very wealthy and Ella was due to inherit the estate on her sixteenth birthday. But her stepmother was not happy that her own daughter would be left with nothing so they hatched a plan to be rid of Ella for good.

So the stepsister took to her bed feigning illness.

'Primroses,' she declared, 'were all she needed, the beautiful scent would raise her spirits and make her well again.'

The stepmother hurried down the worn stone steps to the kitchen 'Ella get your coat, you must go out and find some primroses for your poor sister. I think she will die if she does not have them.'

Ella was dismayed, it was the middle of the winter with deep snow on the ground.

'I wish to help my sister, but it is too early for primroses,' she said.

The stepmother would not listen and pushed her out of the door into the cold, hoping that Ella would become lost and die in the snow.

Wrapping her jacket about her, Ella pushed her hands deep into her pockets and headed towards the forest. In the spring the floor of the forest was thick with primroses but now there was only snow beneath the trees.

Dusk began to fall but in the forest it was very dark and Ella became so cold that she lost all feeling in her fingers and toes. She desperately wanted to go home but dare not without the flowers. Just as she was giving up hope she saw a glow off in the trees. Gathered around the flames was the Council of the Faerie Seasons; too cold to feel afraid Ella stumbled forward and asked if she could warm herself by their fire.

'Come forward child and warm yourself,' Faerie Spring beckoned her forward. 'Why do you disturb our council? '

Ella explained her search for the flowers for her sick sister.

'I will help you,' said the Spring Faerie. 'As you have such a pure soul.' She lent over and breathed gently on the snow covered ground and from under the mantle of ice six beautiful primrose blooms appeared.

'Thank you so much,' Ella said gathering them carefully, and hurried back through the dark forest to her home.

The stepmother's face when she answered the door to Ella! She snatched the flowers from Ella's hand and sent her back down to the kitchen.

That night the stepsister took to her bed again declaring that she was ill. 'What I really need are strawberries, something to tempt my appetite and make me well again.'

The stepmother hurried down the worn stone steps to the kitchen. 'Ella get your coat, you must go out and find some strawberries for your poor sister, I am sure she will die if she does not have them.'

'I wish to help my poor sister, but it is much too early for strawberries,' she said.

The front door shut, with a bang behind Ella leaving her alone in the cold once again.

Ella hurried back into the forest, to find the Council of Faeries, hoping that they would help her again. Far off she could see their fire burning brightly.

'Please may I warm myself by your fire again?'

The Summer Faerie beckoned her forward. 'Come child and what do you seek now?'

'Strawberries for my sick sister otherwise she is sure to die.'

'I will help you,' said the Summer Faerie. 'As you have such a kind heart".'

The faerie opened her hand and inside nestled in a basket of leaves were four large strawberries.

Thanking the faeries Ella hurried home.

Her stepmother was amazed that she had come back but the stepsister was delighted with the fruit and ate them all quickly.

'They are so delicious, why didn't you bring more?' she asked greedily.

All the next day her stepsister lay on her bed complaining how ill she was.

'Apples! I need apples,' she exclaimed. 'And tell her to bring more this time.'

The stepmother hurried down the worn stone steps to the kitchen.

'Ella get your coat, you must go out and find some apples for your poor sister, I know she will die if she does not have them.'

'I wish to help my poor sister, but it is really too early for apples,' she protested.

So Ella set off to the forest again, struggling through the snow until she could see the faerie's fire in the distance.

'Please help me kind faeries for now my stepsister wants apples.'

The faeries smiled and beckoned her forward into the warmth of the fire.

'I will help you,' said the Autumn Faerie. 'As you are so patient.'

The faerie walked to a nearby tree and caressed the bark, whispering words of enchantment to the spirit of the tree within. And on a branch over Ella's head two small apples appeared which grew and grew until they were big and ripe.

She carefully picked them and put them into her apron pocket. 'Thank you so much,' she said politely and hurried home.

The stepmother was most disappointed to see Ella back but her stepsister was delighted with the apples and snatched them quickly, exclaiming at the delicious flavour.

Her stepmother took a bite of the second apple. 'Why didn't you get more of this wonderful fruit?' she scolded Ella, but Ella was not listening. She was so tired that she had fallen asleep in a chair by the fire.

'Come daughter, let us go and find some more apples ourselves.'

They wrapped themselves up against the cold and set off for the forest. The snow was deep and they became increasingly cold and weary until at last they saw a fire in the distance. The four faeries were gathered around the fire watching as the two figures stumbled into the clearing.

'Out of the way and let us near the fire, for we are freezing.'

The stepmother pushed her way past the Winter Faerie to warm her hands over the flames but as she and her daughter huddled closer to the burning logs the fire slowly died and dwindled down to ash.

'You didn't say please,' said the Winter Faerie, and as she spoke the wind whipped up a blizzard of freezing snow and ice which engulfed the two mortals. The snow piled up high around them and they froze into two solid lumps of ice, still holding out their hands to the fire.

As for Ella, needless to say, she lived happily ever after!

Valerian

This plant is also known as 'allheal' as it has been used for thousands of years as a medicinal herb.

Hang sachets of ground root about the house and this will protect against lightening strikes and evil spirits.

The ground root can also be sprinkled on the floor around two people arguing as this will calm and soothe the atmosphere.

Place in pillows for newlyweds as it arouses amorous feelings.

An oil prepared from valerian and aniseed is said to be used by gypsies to calm unfriendly dogs and soothe skittish horses.

The scent of the plant attracts rats and cats which proved useful for the Pied Piper of Hamelin as he filled his pockets with valerian to lure the rats out of the town.

In 1284 the town of Hamelin in Germany suffered from a plague of rats, so a rat catcher was hired by the townspeople to solve the problem. The Piper arrived in the town wearing his brightly coloured clothes and began to play on his magic pipe to lure the rats away. He led them all the way through the town out to the banks of the Weser River and then into the water where all the rats drowned.

The townspeople were very grateful to be rid of the rats but unwisely refused to pay the Piper, using poverty as an excuse. The Piper was furious and vowed to have his revenge on the town; he then disappeared and the townspeople hoped and believed that he had left for good. But the Piper had not gone, he had camped outside the town and waited until it was St John's Day and the people of the town were gathered in the church. He started to play his magic flute and lured the town's one hundred and thirty children away from the town all the way up Koppelberg Hill where a doorway had opened in the rocks. The children were never seen again, some believed that the door was an entrance into the land of faerie. Only three children remained behind in the town, one child was lame and could not keep up with the Piper, the second child was deaf so could not hear the enchanted music played by the Piper and the last child was blind and could not see to follow the Piper and other children.

Valerian A common native perennial found throughout Britain on rough grassland and scrubby areas. Flowers June to August.

To prepare the root, which has sedative properties, slice and leave to dry slowly. Once thoroughly dry it can be ground and stored in a screw top jar.

Valerian Tea

Blend 1tsp 5ml of dried powdered root in a cup of warm milk. Add honey or brown sugar as required as the root has a strong taste, or alternatively mix ½ oz 12g of dried root with 1oz 25g of fresh mint leaves. Pour over 1 pt 600ml of boiled water and leave 2 hours before straining. Can be drunk warm or cold but no more than three times daily.

This is a good drink to have before bedtime as it is a natural sleeping remedy, good for stress and has no harmful side effects.

The top of the plant is full of phosphorous and is a good addition to the compost heap as it quickly rots down.

Vervain

Vervain was the chief ingredient in an ointment made by witches to make themselves invisible. The ointment would be prepared according to instructions given by the Devil. The other ingredients of the potion was said to be the fat of human babies killed before baptism, belladonna, hemlock and bat's blood. The plant was crushed and steeped in olive oil or lard then squeezed through a cloth to remove the leaves and stems. It was applied to the body while using incantations, this would make it possible for the witches to travel to and fro to their covens in secret.

Wear a charm of this plant around your neck if you are troubled with headaches , it will also guard against snake bites and bring you good luck.

Chant this while gathering the herb:

'Allheal- thou holy herb, Vervain
Growing on the ground,
Blessed is that place
Whereon thou art found'

Vervain *A native perennial of roadsides and waste ground. Common in southern England and Wales rarer elsewhere. Flowers June to Sept.*

The plant has many uses such as treating nervous disorders, staunching wounds and aiding childbirth.

Vervain Tea

Take 1 tsp 5 ml of dried vervain or 1 heaped tsp 5 ml of fresh leaves and flowers, place in a cup and pour on boiling water. Leave to steep for 10 minutes then strain and serve. It has a bitter taste but the addition of honey makes it more palatable.

Vervain is an anti-depressant and is good for convalescents and depression; it also encourages the production of breast milk.

Gypsy Love Potion

One single elecampane plant, a handful of vervain leaves, a handful of fennel and a small quantity of grated ginger. Heat these in the oven until they are dry and crumbly then grind into a powder. Add one pinch to a glass of hot mulled wine. If you drink this you will experience unbridled passion.

Mandrake

This is a poisonous perennial herb and is a member of the nightshade family, it has powerful magical properties. The root, which resembles the figure of a man or woman, has a strong unpleasant odour and is used in philtres as an aphrodisiac.

In medieval times it was believed that the mandrake grew best beneath a gallows tree as the roots would spring up from the semen and other body fluids of the hanged corpse. The gallows were traditionally placed at cross roads, a place long associated with magic and evil. Animals would be sacrificed here in honour of Hecate, the goddess of witchcraft, and it was here that witches would call up devils and demons, as certain spells were considered to be more effective if cast at a crossroad.

The corpses of the condemned would be cut down and buried here as it was believed that their ghosts would be confused by the choice of roads and be unable to find their way home.

Local witches would gather the roots of the mandrake at night for use in their spells. The roots would be washed in wine and wrapped in silk and velvet and fed on sacraments stolen from a church.

To harvest the root is not easy, the plant will shriek when approached and to just touch it would be fatal and whoever pulls up the root will die in agony.

To harvest it safely dig around the root, leaving a small part still in the ground. Then tie a dog to the remaining root with a piece of rope and walk away. The dog will try to follow and as it does so it will strangle itself while pulling the plant from the ground. The death of the dog adds to the power of the mandrake and gives it the power to protect against demons.

Witches use a spell to give the mandrake the ability to speak; they cover the root in human blood and give it eyes and a mouth using berries. If the spell works the mandrake will be able to give information about the future by shaking its head in answer to questions and give the location of hidden treasure.

The root contains a powerful alkaloid which will cause hallucinations and delirium; too large a dose will induce a coma. It was used as a surgical anaesthetic as early as AD 60.

It was believed that the root would protect against battle wounds, would cure all diseases, bring luck in love, and promote fertility (to do this sleep with it under your pillow)

To add to the myths surrounding the plant, the berries glow in the light of the dawn as the chemical substances in the berries react with the dew to produce a pale light.

Witches were known to take the right hand of the hanged man, preferably a murderer, as this would be a powerful tool to be used in magic. The hand had to be taken before the corpse was cut down from the gallows but doing this was very dangerous as it would alert the authorities that a witch was in the vicinity. The hand would be wrapped in a piece of shroud, squeezed to remove the blood and fluid then pickled with salt, long peppers and salt petre. It would be kept in this way for two weeks before drying in the oven with vervain. The blood and fluid that had been drained from the hand was mixed with salt and other ingredients, reduced to a dry powder then stuffed back into the hand. Fat from the hand was rendered down and made into candles using the corpse's hair for wicks, the finished candles would be stuck onto the hand between the fingers.

These would be lit when the witches were mixing a particularly evil brew as it intensified the potion.

The candles were often bought from the witches by thieves as they believed that by using the 'Hand of Glory' they could immobilise the occupants of any household and render them speechless while they robbed the house. This is recounted in The Ingoldsby Legends by Thomas Ingoldsby.

The thieves lit the Hand of Glory before entering the house; if the thumb refused to burn it meant that somebody was still awake inside and that they could not be charmed.

Once the hand was lit nothing could extinguish it except milk. An ointment made from the blood of a screech owl, the fat of white hens and the bile of black cats could be used as a counter charm by smearing it on the threshold.

Rosemary

This is a herb of remembrance and fidelity; a sprig of rosemary was put into bridal bouquets or worn at a funeral. Rosemary was also placed in the hands of a corpse; this practice carried on up until the early 20th century.

This herb will ward of infection and protect you from the forces of evil; planting a rosemary bush by your door will purge the house of evil influences and keep out witches. During the middle ages the herb was used during exorcisms to smoke out the devil while in Portugal the rosemary is dedicated to the faeries.

If you suffer from bad dreams place a sprig under your pillow and drink a cup of rosemary tea at night. This will calm your nerves, help you to sleep and aid digestion.

Rosemary can also be used on St Valentine's day to find out your true love. Before you start you must fast for a day, then place several yarrow and rosemary leaves upon your pillow then sprinkle with rose water and retire for the night uttering this incantation:

'Sweet valentine, favour me
In a dream let me my true love see.'

During the night your future lover will appear; if the leaves are still fresh in the morning the relationship will prosper.

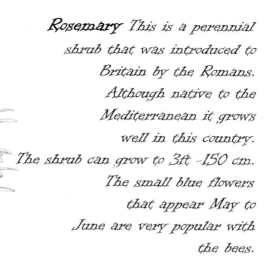

Rosemary This is a perennial shrub that was introduced to Britain by the Romans. Although native to the Mediterranean it grows well in this country. The shrub can grow to 3ft -150 cm. The small blue flowers that appear May to June are very popular with the bees.

Rosemary has the power to make the old young again, as an old Queen found out. She longed for her youth so that she might once again go dancing. So 'of Rosemary she took six pounde, and grounde it well in a stounde and then mixed it with water in which she bathed three times a day, taking care to anoint her head with the goode balm.' A short time after, her old flesh fell away and she became young again. She then started to cast her eye about for a young husband to go dancing with.

Rosemary Oil

2/3 pt 400 ml almond oil

1 tbsp 15ml white wine vinegar

A sprig of fresh bruised rosemary

Fill a bottle with the almond oil and vinegar and place the rosemary inside. Leave the bottle on a sunny windowsill for 3-4 weeks.

The oil can then be used when needed, adding it to your bath will help to ease aches and pains.

The oil will also help take away marks, spots and scars in the skin.

96

Hair Conditioner

For dandruff and a cure for baldness *

1 bunch of chopped rosemary in ½ pt 300 ml of boiling water, allow to stand for 1 hour then strain. Use as a rinse after washing hair.

* There is no cure for the hereditary male pattern baldness but for temporary hair loss due to illness or stress etc the use of this conditioner or rubbing oil of rosemary into the scalp will help with the problem.

If you have dry hair place 1 oz 25 g of rosemary in 1 pt 600 ml of olive oil and let it stand for one week on a sunny windowsill. When ready massage the oil into the scalp, wrap a warm towel around your hair and leave for 10 minutes. Do this before washing the hair.

Rosemary Tea

Crush 1 tbsp 15 ml rosemary leaves and place in a cup of boiling water, allow to steep for 5 minutes before drinking. Also good for tension, nervous headaches and depression.

This herb also makes an excellent skin tonic when made into an oil, it can be used in embrocations and rubbing oils to stimulate the skin, increase the circulation and will help calm the nerves.

long time ago when all things were possible, a Queen of Italy gave birth to a rosemary bush. She protected it and tended it most carefully for many years and it grew in to a beautiful fragrant bush which held a secret only the Queen knew. All was well until one year the young King of Spain visited the King and Queen of Italy. He spied the beautiful bush in the Queen's private garden and desired it for his own palace, so the young man crept into the garden that night and stole the bush, taking it back to Spain with him.

It thrived in his sunny garden and he spent many pleasant days admiring the fragrant plant. One fine day while sitting near it he started to play on his flute, as the notes of his melody wafted about the garden he heard a rustling in the rosemary bush and a beautiful Princess appeared from amongst the leaves. Her name was Rosa Marina and she was the daughter of the Queen of Italy.

The King helped her step from the bush and sat her down on the marble bench, looking at her beautiful face he quickly fell in love. The King visited her every day, playing his flute to call her forth from the bush. After several weeks of meeting in the garden the King was even more deeply in love and wished to marry Rosa Marina but news came of a war in the north of his kingdom before he could do so. The King could not take Rosa Marina with him but resolved to marry her on his return. He left strict instructions with his head gardener that no harm should come to the rosemary bush and every care and attention must be given to the plant.

The King rode away to war convinced that all would be well.

The gardener tended the bush carefully until one evening the King's sisters decided to take their flutes into the cool garden to play. On hearing the music Rosa Marina appeared. The sisters were astonished to see this beautiful girl emerge from a bush in the garden. Angry and jealous that their brother had concealed this girl they fell upon Rosa Marina, beating her and attacking the bush. The Princess vanished and the bush immediately began to wilt. The gardener was horrified when he saw the rosemary bush; he knew that the King would be furious and punish him for the damage.

The man tried everything to revive the plant but each day more leaves fell from the dying bush and nothing he did made any difference. At his wit's end, he entered the palace library and searched through all the books looking for something to help him. At last he found what he needed, an old book covered in dust on one of the top shelves. Inside was a piece written about the magical properties of dragon's blood and how a few drops could restore life to all things.

The gardener hurried to the palace stables to saddle his mule and taking some food from the kitchens he set off for the mountains. After a long hard journey through the high crags he spied a huge dragon sunning itself on the warm rocks far above. The gardener took the dagger from his belt and crept closer to the sleeping dragon's tail. Here the skin was soft and pink and he would be able to draw the blood he needed.

He made a small nick in the tip of the dragon's tail and held a little wooden cup under the wound. With each drop of blood into the cup the dragon stirred. By the time the fourth drop of blood had been collected the dragon was nearly awake. It began to yawn and stretch, and the frightened gardener crept slowly and carefully away before the beast noticed the cut on his tail. Tucking the cup carefully inside his jerkin he hurried back down the rocky trail to his waiting mule.

The four drops of blood were poured over the roots of the rosemary bush and it began to revive almost immediately; the damaged branches re-grew and before long it looked as healthy as the day the King had left. It was just beginning to flower as the trumpets sounded and the King himself rode through the gates of the city.

He hurried to his garden to see that all was well with the Princess and as she came forth from the bush he realised that he loved her so much that he immediately asked her to marry him.

Hearing their brother's arrival the sisters hurried to the garden to greet him and were dismayed to see that Rosa Marina had returned. They were even more dismayed when the King, learning of their cruelty, banished his sisters from the kingdom. He married his Princess and they both lived happily ever after. The sisters weren't so lucky however, they wandered into the mountains looking for food and shelter and were eaten by a very angry dragon.

Snail

Here are a few traditional remedies using snails, however, I would not recommend these as it seems rather hard on the poor snails!

To cure cold sores, rub a snail over the sore then seal the snail in a bottle and bury it in the garden. As the snail dies the sore will fade away.

To cure a hangover, rub a snail nine times over your forehead then throw the snail as far as possible.

To cure a wart, take a black snail, rub it over the wart nine times in two directions. The snail should then be impaled upon a blackthorn, as it dies the wart will disappear.

Snail juice was also considered to be an effective treatment for weak backs and ankles; the snails were either boiled and the liquid drunk or twelve snails would be collected, crushed, then hung in a bag. The liquid which dripped from the bag would be collected and rubbed into the weak areas.

In Cornwall, snails were regarded as a lucky charm, especially ones with a striped shell. The snail would be thrown backwards over the finder's head while chanting:

'Lucky snail, lucky snail, go over my head
And bring me a penny before I go to bed.'

The Golden Snail is based on a traditional folktale from Java, it tells of the Princess Dewi who was famed for her beauty throughout her father's kingdom.

Dewi fell in love with Prince Rhaden who lived in a neighbouring kingdom and they were due to be married in a few days time. One afternoon, tired of the hustle and bustle of the wedding preparations, she escaped to the palace gardens and while wandering down one of the many paths she noticed an ugly snail on one of the flowers.

Dewi picked it off in disgust and threw it over the palace wall and into the river beyond. What she didn't realise was the snail was an evil old witch in disguise.

Within minutes the hag came screaming back over the wall on her broomstick, dripping wet and her eyes blazing with fury.

'How dare you!' she screamed. 'You'll pay for this.' The Princess cowered away from her. 'I'm sorry, I didn't realise,' as she spoke she began to feel very strange. 'No!' she wailed.

By the time the witch had finished weaving her spell the Princess had disappeared and a beautiful golden snail lay on the path in her place.

The old woman grinned spitefully, picked up the snail and sent it flying over the wall, far out into the river.

104

The snail bobbed slowly downstream until it reached the mouth of the river. On the shore a lone figure was fishing. The current caught the drifting snail and carried it straight into the man's net.

The fisherman pulled the net up onto the sand but it was empty of fish, all he had caught that day was a tangled mess of seaweed and the snail. It lay there glinting in the sun.

Why, he thought, it looks just like gold.

He picked it up and decided to take it home for his ailing wife. Popping it into his pocket he gathered up the nets and set off for home.

His wife was delighted with her gift, she held it up to the light where it glinted and sparkled.

'Its so pretty,' she said weakly and popped it into a jar next to the bed where she lay.

'Just bread and water for supper I am afraid dear,' he said straightening the blankets over his wife.

'That's alright Tomas, I'm not hungry.' She laid back on her pillows and closed her eyes.

'I'll catch some fish tomorrow you will see.'

By sunrise the next day Tomas was already on his way to the shore. He spent all day fishing, on either side his neighbours were pulling in nets full of fish but nothing found their way into his. Tomas sighed wearily but carried on long after the others had packed up and gone home. It was nearly dark by the time he had trudged home, resigned to another supper of bread.

But as he pushed open the door a great tide of fish slithered out of the door.

'What is all this?' he called to his wife who was sitting up in bed with the blanket clutched under her chin.

'I don't know where they came from and somebody has cleaned and tidied the cottage,' she wailed.

That night the old couple had the first decent meal they'd had for months; they both ate until they could eat no more and still had plenty of fish left over.

'I'll pack up the rest of the fish in the morning and take them into town.'

His wife settled back on her pillows. 'I feel so much better,' she said sleepily and started to gently snore.

Early the next morning, just before it got light, Tomas packed the fish into rush baskets.

'I'll see you later, wife.' He shouldered the baskets and set off down the rough track to the market.

The old woman watched her husband out of the window until she could only just make out his figure walking away towards the village.

Behind her there was a small plop.

The snail had dropped off the table onto the cottage floor where it began to grow and grow until it became the size of a large pumpkin. The shell rocked backwards and forwards, first one arm and then another appeared in the entrance to the shell. The old woman watched in amazement as with a huffing and puffing, a young woman crawled out of the shell. She stood up with a sigh and smoothed down her dress.

'Why, who are you?' stammered the old woman

'Oh you're awake this morning, you looked so tired yesterday that I didn't like to disturb you.'

'You brought all the fish? Who are you?' she asked again.

'I'm Princess Dewi. An evil old Witch cast a spell on me and I can only turn back into my human form for an hour at sunrise.'

The Princess busied herself about, as she talked, she tidied the table and swept the floor then returned to the snail shell on the floor and kneeling in front of it pulled out handfuls of fish and placed them on the table.

'That is so kind of you Princess, my husband has taken some of the fish to the market to sell.' The old woman watched from her bed as the young woman prepared the fish for a stew. 'If only we could help you.'

'The curse can only be lifted by my future husband Prince Rhaden, he must obtain a few drops of the witch's blood, sprinkle them on the shell and then break it.'

'Well then, a message must be taken to the Prince to let him know that you are here.'

She watched all day for her husband to return from the market. The old woman was getting very impatient by the time she spied him slowly walking up the track. Tomas was laden down with bundles and packages. He'd had a good day at the market. Inside she showed him the fish lying on the table and told him all about the events of the morning.

'You must go to the palace and find the Prince.'

'The Princess is in there?' he asked, picking up the shell and peering inside.

'Yes, yes,' she said and pushed him out of the door. 'Now do as you are told old man and go to the palace.'

Rhaden was overjoyed to find out the fate of his beloved Dewi and hurried back to the fisherman's hut with the old man. He picked up the beautiful golden snail and kissed it. The Prince could not thank the elderly couple enough before carrying the shell carefully back to the palace.

'Now don't forget,' the old woman called after him. 'The curse can only be broken by the witch's blood.'

Back at the palace Prince Rhaden placed the golden snail on a velvet cushion next to the throne and sat down.

'Find the witch and bring her here at once,' he ordered the palace guard.

The witch was dragged in screaming, her arms held firmly by her sides by the guards.

'At last, bring her here.'

She was hauled in front of the prince spluttering curses.

'Silence witch, the Princess has been returned to us, now you must restore her to her former self.'

'Never!' she screamed.

The Prince drew a dagger and approached the old woman. 'Give me some of your blood, witch.'

'No!, no!' she shouted and wrenched her arms away from the guards. 'Now you'll be sorry! I will change you into a snail as well!' She raised her arms to weave an enchantment but a guard drew his sword and lunged forward. The witch was too quick and ran towards the window and threw herself out; just before she disappeared the prince managed to nick her ankle with his dagger, and caught three drops of her blood on the blade.

Rhaden carried the dagger carefully over to the snail and sprinkled the blood over it,, but before he could pick it up and smash the shell the witch came flying back in through the broken window.

'No you don't,' she screamed and tried to snatch the shell away from the Prince. Rhaden held in firmly in his cupped hands and backed away from the furious witch.

'Guards,' he shouted. 'Take her prisoner.'

The guards advanced on the scrawny figure but before they could pin her down she turned them all into large green frogs.

'Now it's your turn,' she snarled, turning to the prince and flexing her fingers. He looked at the frogs hopping about the palace floor and turned and fled for the door. He slammed and locked it behind him but it shattered into a thousand pieces as the witch appeared in the doorway.

The Prince ran towards the staircase with the old hag hard on his heels.

'Give me that shell,' she screamed, trying to snatch it from his hand.

As Rhaden ran up the stairs, he could feel her trying to grab his ankles.

'Get off you hag,' he shouted as he reached the top and headed out onto the balcony. The young man drew back his arm to throw the shell onto the flagstone below.

'No! I will give you anything you could wish for, just do not smash it,' the old woman pleaded.

He hesitated for a moment, worried that Dewi would not survive the fall. The wily old witch saw the doubt on his face. 'That's right, Dewi will be hurt if you throw the snail down into the courtyard. Give it to me and I will change her back.'

Rhaden hesitated and then caught sight of the evil look on the witch's face.

'No,' he said and threw the snail over the railings, as it fell the shell grew in size and by the time it hit the ground it was the size of a large pumpkin. The shell cracked in two and out crawled the Princess. Behind Rhaden there was another sharp crack. He turned and saw in amazement the witch slowly changing into a snail herself. Rhaden leapt over the rapidly dwindling figure and ran down the stairs to find the Princess.

'Dewi, thank goodness you're alright.'

'I knew you would break the spell and rescue me! What happened to the witch?'

'Her spell has been broken and she has been turned into an ugly old snail!'

The happy couple were married the next day and the most welcome guests there were old Tomas and his wife.

There were reports of an ugly snail being seen in the palace gardens for several days after the wedding but the Prince was taking no chances and ordered that all snails were to be removed from the garden and destroyed.

Honeysuckle

Honeysuckle will protect your garden against evil as it is a barrier to witches; either grow it in the garden or place a sprig over your door. Hang some honeysuckle over the cattle shed or stables as this will benefit the animals too.

This plant is also known as 'lovebind' due to its clinging growing habits. It symbolizes a lover's embrace and will bring them all good luck.

In Scotland a honeysuckle stick was vital when courting, it would bring luck to the relationship and indicate that the young man's intentions were honourable.

If the flowers are brought into the house, a wedding is sure to follow as the fragrance induces dreams of love and passion.

Honeysuckle A native shrub very common in woods, hedges and scrub land. Found throughout Britain. Its trailing stems can grow up to 18ft-6m.
Flowers June to September.
The berries appear Aug to September.

114

There are over 100 species of honeysuckle but only about a dozen are used medicinally.

The flowers have a natural anti-histamine effect and are used for external applications for the treatment of skin infections. The flowers can be combined with mint for skin rashes and other skin problems brought on by stress.

The **berries** of the honeysuckle are poisonous.

Honeysuckle Tea

Add ½ tsp 2 ½ ml of fresh washed flowers to one cup of green tea.

The leaves and flowers are rich in salicylic acid which is similar to aspirin so this tea is beneficial for headaches, fevers, bronchial problems and rheumatism; also useful for hot flushes during the menopause. As the honeysuckle is antiseptic it can be used for treating sore throats.

Honeysuckle in Honey

Place fresh clean honeysuckle flowers in a jar then fill with a runny honey. Place this on a sunny windowsill and leave for 2 weeks. Make sure the flowers are kept immersed in the honey otherwise they will go brown. After the 2 weeks strain then bottle. Take 1 teaspoonful as needed.

 * The honey contains healing properties as well, see page 116.

For Chillblains: Honeysuckle in Oil

Pick several heads of the honeysuckle and detach the flowerets.

Place in a bowl and pour over 2 floz 50ml hot almond oil, allow to cool and then sieve.

The warm oil can then be applied to the chillblains. Store the oil in a cool dark place, then gently reheat when needed.

Bees

These insects need to feed nearly all year long, February until October; so flowers in the garden are really important to the bees and other insects.

Honeybees and bumble bees all produce honey to feed their young and while doing so pollinate the plants.

The honey they produce as well as tasting nice has medicinal uses as well. The wound healing properties of honey has been recognised for over 3,000 years.

The honey contains an enzyme which produces hydrogen peroxide which disinfects and helps to heal wounds rapidly with minimal scarring.

Propolis is a resinous substance created by the bees to seal cracks and holes in their hives. It has been found that this substance has powerful antibiotic properties and is used in the treatment of flu, respiratory problems, tonsillitis, laryngitis and mouth ulcers. It raises the body's natural resistance to infection by stimulating the immune system.

Pollen is another useful byproduct of the bees industry, it is used as a super food, ideal for anaemia, anorexia and fatigue. But its main use is for the treatment of hayfever. Chewing on a honeycomb is a traditional remedy for the problem; can be effective for other allergies and sinusitis.

Bee stings have anti-inflammatory compounds and are being looked at as a treatment for joint problems as it is well known that beekeepers do not suffer from arthritis!

There is much folklore surrounding bees, one of the most common is that the bees must be told all the important news of the household, by tapping on the hive with a key or by whispering the news.

The bees must be told when the head of the household dies or they will fly away to find them:

> 'Bees Bees awake
> Your master is dead
> And another you must take'

The hives must be turned or moved as the corpse leaves the house for burial.

If you wish to purchase a hive for your garden do not pay for them with money but in goods, wheat, oats etc. A bought swarm will bring nothing but bad luck to your new venture, and do not move them over running water as they will not survive long after this. The new hive will thrive in a happy atmosphere as they dislike a quarrelsome house, but if the bees do suddenly depart it is a sure sign that the owner will shortly die.

Bumble bees have a few myths attached to them as well; the fishermen on the Isle of Man catch the first bumble bee of spring and take it out fishing with them as it brings good luck and will ensure a good catch.

A bumble bee coming into the house means that a stranger will soon be visiting you and if a witch swallows a queen bee before she is arrested she will be able to withstand the torture during the trial without confessing.

Philtres

A philtre usually consists of wine, tea or water infused with herbs or drugs.

These would have been concocted by a witch or wise women and is most effective if mixed at the start of the waxing moon. Philtres have been used for hundreds of years but started to decline in favour as spells and charms became more popular for healing. Using philtres was forbidden under Anglo Saxon law and anybody found with them were dealt with quite severely, in fact anything to do with magic was frowned upon.

The most common ingredient for a philtre would have been mandrake root along with vervain, briony and fern seeds. Orange, honey and ambergis would have been added to the final mixture in an effort to disguise the unpleasant taste of the mandrake.

Philtres could also be baked into a cake. The sweat of the spell caster must be collected from their body by rubbing themselves with flour. This would then be mixed with oil, egg and the ashes of their burnt hair, collected from every part of the body, then baked. This cake would be fed to the object of the person's lust.

Medieval Love Potion

Grind into powder the heart of a dove, the liver of a sparrow, the womb of a swallow and the kidney of a hare. To this add equal parts of the persons own blood, also dried and powdered. Mix into liquid and offer to the intended to drink. Supposed to be most effective.

St Johns Wort

This plant blooms during the summer solstice and is at its most powerful on 24th June, St John's day. On this day it would be ceremonially burnt on bonfires in honour of the festival.

It is very powerful against faerie spells and will protect against demons, witches and evil spirits hence its ancient name of *Fuga Daemonum*.

'St John's Wort doth charm all the witches away
If gathered at midnight on the Saint's Holy day
And Devils and Witches have no power to harm
Those that do gather the plant for a charm
Rub the lintels and the post with that red juicy flower
No thunder no tempest will then have the power
To hurt or hinder your house: and bind
Round your neck a charm of similar kind'

Perforate St John's Wort

A native perennial found
growing singly or in clumps
at the edges of woodland,
hedges, grassland and
roadside verges.
Likes full sun or semi shade.
Flowers May to September.

Slender St John's Wort

A native perennial, found in hedges,
rough grassland and woods.
Common in Britain.
Flowers June to August.

There are approximately 370 species of the genus
hypericum to which St John's Wort belongs.
Originally indigenous to Europe but it has been
introduced to many temperate countries. It grows so
successfully that it has become a serious problem to
livestock causing stomach problems, drowsiness etc,
and is now considered to be a noxious weed. In
western North America beetles have been introduced
to try and control the spread of the plant.

The plant is imbued with magical powers and can be used for divination but gathering the flowers can be difficult as it is said that the plant will move away from anybody trying to pick it.

Traditionally young girls would pick the flowers in an attempt to predict their married state; if the flowers remained fresh till the morning their chances of happiness were good but if the plant was wilted their future would be dismal.

The plant is also dangerous to step on. If you are careless enough to step on a flower during the day faeries will whisk you away on a wild ride across the countryside and then drop you in a ditch miles from anywhere. Stepping on a flower just before bedtime will ensure that you are kept awake all night by mischievous elves, but to ensure a good night's sleep, with no bad dreams, place a sprig of the plant along with some thyme under your pillow.

St John's Wort Tea

This is a good remedy for depression, influenza and incontinence but on a note of caution, the herb can have a few side effects and may cause sensitivity to light.

Pour 2 cups of boiling water over 1 oz 25 g of the dried herb and steep for 10 to 20 minutes. You can add honey or lemon if you like or for a cold day try adding cinnamon or cloves. Drink 3 to 4 cups a day.

St John's Wort Oil

Pick the flowering tops of the plant on a fine day and pound down with a pestle and mortar, moisten it all with a drop of vegetable oil. Put the mix into a screw top jar and cover with more vegetable oil, shake the mixture thoroughly and stand on a sunny windowsill. Shake every day until the oil changes into a deep red colour. Strain and pour into a new clean jar and then the mixture can be used when needed.

This oil can be used for healing wounds, burns and sores, also good for a massage oil for back pain. It is an analgesic and anti-inflammatory and is good for fibrositis, neuralgia, sciatica, rheumatism, gout and arthritis.

Poppet

Poppets, also known as mommets, are lifelike figures usually made of cloth but can be of clay, wax, straw etc. They are made to represent a certain person and by adding their hair, toenail clippings saliva etc, it reinforces the bond between the poppet and the intended recipient. Life must be breathed into the doll and the doll then named.

Poppets are used in ritual magic and spell craft and have been in use for thousands of years, they are very similar to the voodoo doll but are of much older origin.

In ancient Greece they were known as 'Kolossos' and were used for binding, healing and defence of family and home. The Babylonians used poppets for defensive magic, placing them at entrances to their homes. The dolls were also used for this purpose by the Egyptians; spells were written on the clay poppets which were then broken and buried.

These dolls are a good example of sympathetic magic, which works on two laws. The law of similarity: this states that like produces like, so the poppet is made to represent and therefore substitute a certain person. The law of contact states that whatever is done to the object affects the person to whom the poppet is linked.

Most important is the power of the intent, good or ill, of the person who has made the poppet as this will bring a successful outcome to the spell.

Today they are used more in healing, fertility and protection spells.

Healing Poppet

(Positive magic is done under a waxing moon)

First make a lifelike figure in white cloth or felt, and if possible, try to add some material from a garment of the recipient. Stuff the doll with calendula, lavender, rosemary, lemon balm, feverfew, ivy and pine, add some of their hair, nail clippings, saliva etc, a photo can be added if you have one. Then place either a rose quartz, clear crystal, bloodstone or turquoise inside the poppet as near to the heart as possible. Then seal the doll. If the intended is recovering from surgery make an incision in the appropriate place.

Life must be breathed into the doll using a straw to blow into the poppet's mouth saying:

'Though separate you were,
Now you are one,
The link of unison has begun.

The poppet must then be named:

'Image of health, thy purpose is healing (or love)
I give you the name of.............
Their body is your body
Their health is your health
I proclaim you one.'

Light a candle and visualize the person healthy and full of life, remember it is your strength of will and intent that is the most important part of the spell.

Chant three times:

'Herbs of healing
The body is free of pain
The soul is free
The mind is free
whole and healed
With harm to none
My will is done
So mote it be!'

There are different views of what to do next with the poppet, bury the doll prior to sunset on the same day, pull the poppet apart and destroy it completely or give it to the intended recipient. I think you have to be guided by your own instincts on this.

Love Poppet

Follow the instructions for the Healing Poppet but use a pink material instead which will bring fertility, love and compassion.

Stuff the poppet with lavender, rose, patchouli, basil parsley, and peppermint. Use lapis lazuli, malachite, jade or rose quartz. Include hair and nail clippings etc plus stitch a heart to the outside of the doll.

Breath life into the doll and name.

Once that is done you can cast your spell.

Chant three times:

'Truelove and desire shall come to me
God and Goddess make it be.'

Remember this is to attract love, not to bind somebody.

Autumn

'Come' said the wind to
The leaves one day,
'Come o're the meadows
And we will play,
Put on your dresses
Scarlet and gold
For summer is gone
And the days grow cold'

Traditional children's song

The apple symbolises fruitfulness, prosperity, and rejuvenation and the wood is still seen as a symbol of security. Beware of entering an apple orchard as the trees are inhabited by faeries and pixies, so do not sit beneath a tree and fall asleep or you will fall under a faerie enchantment. If you wish to call upon the faeries summon them with an apple wood wand; and eating an enchanted apple will allow you to enter the faerie realm.

The oldest tree in the orchard is inhabited by the Apple Tree Man, who is the guardian of the orchard. To honour him the last few apples must be left for him and the pixies; this custom is called griggling, pixy hoarding and cullpixying.

Burn the bark as an offering to the faeries on midsummer night.

In Somerset and Dorset the orchards are guarded by the colt, Lazy Lawrence, while in Yorkshire it is Auld Goggie who stands guard over the trees.

Apple is one of the most widely cultivated fruit trees and the earliest. There are hundreds of different cultivars. Alexander the Great was reputed to have found a dwarfed apple variety in Asia Minor in 300 BC.

The crab apple is native to Britain and is a familiar hedgerow and woodland tree. It is the ancestor of all the cultivated varieties and supplied the stock on which all choice trees were grafted. These were probably introduced by the Romans; by the time of the Norman Conquest many apple varieties were abundant in Britain.

One common belief is that the apple has many magical and healing properties and as with most traditional remedies there is a basis for this. The pectin in the apple is a good germicide which promotes healthy skin tissue.

Apple juice applied to the skin cures redness and it was used to treat the redness caused by too much alcohol.

To cure a wart rub a cut apple over it then bury the apple in the garden. As the apple rots the wart will disappear, this remedy was used for rheumatism. The juice of the apple can be used to cure small cuts.

The old saying 'an apple a day keeps the doctor away' shows that our forbears knew what they were doing as the apple is a natural remedy for the stomach; aiding digestion and keeping the bowels regular! It is also good for the heart.

The bark can be used as a tonic and a stimulant; it will help reduce fever.

To use the bark strip a small piece of bark from an apple tree,but be careful not to ring the tree as you might kill it.

Boil the bark in water for 15 minutes and leave to infuse overnight. Take 1-4 fl oz 100-150 ml of the infusion daily.

Boiled or roasted fruit will help with burn marks and it can be applied to sore eyes.

There are many superstitions surrounding apples and orchards, these beliefs were taken seriously in earlier days: felling an apple tree would bring the death penalty as it was believed to bring bad luck.

Apple blossom must not be brought into the house as it will bring sickness and the evil influence, and if blossom appears on a tree late in the season it foretells a death in the family.

'A bloom on the tree when the apples are ripe, Is a sure termination of somebody's life'

The apple symbolises fruitfulness so barren
women would roll on the ground in
orchards in an effort to conceive,
they also believed that wearing pieces
of bark pinned to their clothes would
bring them a child, and if it
was a good year for apples then
they could expect to have twins.
The main tradition of the orchard is the
custom of wassailing the apple trees
during the winter months. This is still
prevalent today and has been revived in many
country areas.

The owner of the orchard, along with friends, gather
in the orchard singing, firing shotguns into the
branches and beating the trunks with sticks to drive
out the evil spirits to ensure a good crop for the
coming year.

Cider is drunk from the wassailing bowl which
contains hot spiced cider, lumps of apple and pieces
of toast.

The remains from the bowl is poured over the roots
as an offering to the Apple Tree Man, and the cider
soaked toast is placed in the forks of the trees.

'Old Apple Tree we wassail thee, and happily thou
wilt bear,
For the Lord knows where we shall be,
Till apples another year'

Lazy Lawrence is a wild colt which inhabits the orchards of the west country; he protects the crops from apple thieves.

There was an elderly widow who had reason to be very grateful for his protection. She lived in a small village in Somerset and owned a fine orchard, from which she made a good living. But one year she fell from one of the apple trees while pruning and was unable to leave her cottage for quite some time. So she called on her nearest neighbour for help but he was a mean spirited man and refused.

Although he would not aid the widow he decided that he would help himself to the apples anyway and perhaps sell them at the local market. The neighbour waited until dark and then crept down the lane carrying a wicker basket. He was so busy picking the apples that he did not notice Lazy Lawrence leap the fence and make straight for the thief. The colt nipped the man in the backside and then chased him round and round the orchard until he collapsed exhausted on the grass under the trees.

The colt pranced up to the man and as he gazed up at the frisking pony its green eyes froze the man to the spot. He was still there the next morning unable to move and next to him was the basket full of stolen apples.

Bramble

To harm the bramble bush is forbidden as it belongs to the faerie folk and the first berries of the season must be left for them. If you do not, then any following fruit that you pick will be rotten and full of maggots.

Even the ancient Celts believed it to be sacred; for them the fruit represented the three aspects of the Goddess: maiden, mother, crone. As the berries changed from white to red then black they believed this signified birth, life and death and the seeds of the fruit were the promise of spring and rebirth.

To keep off evil spirits, pick bramble at the full moon and make a wreath, including rowan and ivy. Hang over the doors to your house; this will protect the inhabitants against evil spells. This belief in the protective qualities of bramble led the plant being planted around fresh graves to protect loved ones against evil, although in some areas it was believed that the bramble would stop the dead rising and returning as ghosts.

If you are troubled by vampires either plant a bramble near to your house or place the berries on the threshold. The vampire will obsessively count the berries and thorns until the first light of day when he will have to depart.

There is a traditional rhyme that goes...

'There was a man in our town,
And he was wondrous wise,
He jumped into a bramble bush,
And scratched out both his eyes....

And when he saw what he had done,
With all his might and main
He jumped into the bramble bush,
And scratched them back again!'

Crawling under the arch of a bramble bush which has formed a second root will cure rheumatism, boils etc. If a child suffers from whooping cough pass it through the arch seven times while chanting:
'In bramble , out cough,
here I leave the whooping cough'

Eating the fruit will help these ailments but remember not to eat them after 10th Oct, 'Devil Blackberry Day,' as the Devil spits on them. When the Devil was kicked out of heaven he fell into a blackberry bush and has hated them ever since. Imps and elves inhabit the bushes and will catch you hair and clothes in the thorns when you try to pick the fruit.

Bramble A common native shrub found throughout Britain. Can climb up to 15ft ~5m. The stems will root where they touch the ground. There are hundreds of micro species in the bramble family. Flowers vary from white to cerise, appearing from May to September. The fruit is a cluster of segments called dropelets and appear in the autumn months and may be seen at the same time as the flowers.

Bramble leaves are used with a **healing spell** for the treatment of burns. Dip nine leaves in running water and lay them on the affected area, say to each leaf as you apply it 'Three ladies came from the east, one with fire and two with frost, out with fire and in with frost'

Or alternatively bruise a handful of fresh leaves and apply to the burn. This can be used for piles, skin ulcers and eczema as well.

Use a decoction of the leaves for sore throats and if you would like a natural mouth wash it can also be used for this.

The juice of the berries mixed with the juice of mulberries binds the stomach in cases of diarrhoea, helps sores and ulcers and is good for piles.

The leaves boiled in lye and used to wash the scalp relieves an itchy scalp and makes the hair black.

Bramble Leaf Tea

The shoots and young leaves are packed with vitamins and minerals and are ideal for use in a tea, either fresh or dried can be used. Place three or four leaves in a teapot and pour on boiling water, leave to steep for about 15 minutes. Strain then drink. This can be taken as needed; if using to treat diarrhoea make the tea twice the strength and take one cup every hour.

Good for mouth ulcers and gum disease, also helpful if you have a cold.

Chewing the leaves will help headaches while crushed leaves treats small wounds and sores.

Bramble Syrup

Cover 1 lb 425g of fresh blackberries with malt vinegar and leave to stand for three days. After which mash the berries then strain.

Add 1 lb 450 g of sugar for each pint of juice that remains and bring to the boil for 5 minutes. Wait until it has cooled then pour into clean jars and seal. One teaspoon can be added to a cup of water and be given to feverish children to help with dehydration.

Blackberry and Apple Jam

3 lbs 1.35 kg blackberries
1 lb 425 g apples (the apples supply the acid and pectin necessary to help jam set)
¼ pt 1.45 water
4 lb 1.8 kg sugar

Cut the apples into pieces leaving the peel and core, cover with water then simmer until soft.

Wash the blackberries thoroughly and add to the apples. Add the sugar and stir until dissolved. Bring to boil and boil rapidly for 10-15 minutes until the jam sets when tested. To test, take a plate that has been in the fridge for 30 minutes and pour a teaspoon of mix onto it, as the jam cools it should set, if not, boil the jam again for a further 10 minutes then test again. Keep doing this until it is of a jam like consistency. (Some batches of jam take more boiling than others)

A dob of butter added to the jam prevents the scum appearing on the top, but if it does, remove before bottling into clean jars. Then seal immediately.

This should make about 6 lbs 2.7 kg of jam.

Winter

No matter how long the winter,
Spring is sure to follow.

This plant brings good luck, fun and happiness, and growing some on the wall of your house will deter misfortune. If you have a house plant of ivy and it dies this might signify that financial problems may be looming.

Ivy was sacred to Bacchus god of wine and to show that good wine could be found within, innkeepers would hang garlands of ivy around their doors.

Ivy is the emblem of fidelity and it was customary to hand a wreath of ivy leaves to newly weds. The bridesmaids would also carry some mixed in with their bouquets as it was believed to aid fertility and bring good luck. Wands entwined with ivy are still used in nature fertility rites and in spells for love magic. (Not to be ingested)

For a man to dream of his future bride he must pick a leaf on the 31st Oct and place it under his pillow.

For a woman to dream of her future husband she must collect some leaves and recite the following:

'Ivy, Ivy I love you,
In my bosom I put you,
The first young man who speaks to me
my future husband he shall be'

If you dream of an ivy plant it may fortel a breakup.

In Shropshire drinking from an ivy cup will cure a child from whooping cough, it will also cure an alcoholic. Placing a trail of ivy leaves across a drunks path will sober him up and bring him to his senses.

Ivy A native perennial climber, the shoots can reach to 90ft- 30m in length.

The flowering shoots have different shaped leaves to the non flowering climbing shoots which are the usual shaped leaf. Flowers September to November, and the fruits appear in November.

The use of ivy as a medicine has been known for hundreds of years. One of the earliest written document from 900 AD describes the use of ivy twigs being boiled in butter for the relief of sunburn and the berries were once recommended as a cure for rheumatism.

There have been a host of other uses for the plant over the years: wearing a garland of ivy leaves around the head was believed to prevent hair loss due to an illness, ivy soaked in vinegar and wrapped around a corn would cure it.

Pressing out the juice from the leaves and taking it up the nostrils would help to cure a cold and streaming nose.

Holly

This is a lucky tree and sacred to the Druids; it symbolises life and immortality. Faeries revere the holly and will take revenge on anybody damaging the tree. The only time it is permissible to cut the holly is on Christmas Eve as it is an important addition to the festive wreath. It was a Celtic custom to gather holly and ivy for decorating the home during the winter, symbolising that life and growth would return.

The faeries and elves would come in with the greenery for shelter during the cold months; in return for shelter they would behave and cause no mischief. However every berry and sprig of holly must be removed from the house by 31st January, Imbolc Eve, otherwise the more mischievous kinds of faeries like goblins will be encouraged to stay.

'Down with the Rosemary and so
Down with the Baies and Mistletoe
Down with the Holly, Ivie and all
Wherewith ye drest the Christmas hall
That so the superstitious find
Not one least branch there left behind
For look how many leaves there be
Neglected there, Maids trust to me
So many Goblins you shall see!'
Robert Hemick

The berries are a witch deterrent and will bring good luck to the house, but the luck diminishes with each berry that falls.

The Holly Man lives in the prickly type of holly and the Holly Woman lives in the smooth variegated type so it is important that equal amounts are brought into the house to ensure domestic harmony for the forthcoming year.

For the protection of the house plant a holly tree outside, although a self seeded one is better, this will bring good luck and protection against storms, lightning, fire and the evil eye. And it is for this reason that holly trees are left uncut in hedges, it prevents witches running along the tops of them.

In Scandinavian mythology, the holly belonged to Thor the God of Thunder hence the belief that the tree would protect against lightening but it is true that holly conducts lightening into the ground better than most trees.

Holly A small native tree or shrub found throughout Britain usually forming part of hedges and woods. The male and female flowers are usually on separate trees and appear from May to August. The red berries appear from September to March and usually persist all winter.

Soaking sprigs of holly in water was used for protection, the water would be sprinkled on newborn babies or anybody who needed protection against witches and the evil eye.

The wood is burnt on ritualistic fires in the making of weapons and tools. Athemes (magical knives) are consecrated in the wood's smoke.

It is used in rituals to help people deal with death and also helps with soothing sleep.

In Celtic lore the Holly King ruled over a half the year from summer to winter then the Oak King defeated him in a great battle to rule from then until the summer solstice when the Holly King would take over again.

The Holly King is depicted as a giant of a man covered in holly leaves and wielding a holly bush as a club.

144

Mistletoe

Mistletoe is a partial parasite and grows on the branches or trunks of a tree, usually an apple or oak. It grows wild only in England and Wales and can grow up to 3ft- 1m in height.

Although the mistletoe will take nutrients from its host plant, it is capable of growing on its own. The small yellow flowers that appear February to April develop into the white sticky berries from November to December. The berries are poisonous but are eaten by the mistle thrush which then carries the seed to a new host tree, (either by wiping the sticky berries off their beaks or by their excrement)

The mistletoe that grows on the oak was sacred to the ancient Celts, it would be cut on the sixth night of the new moon at midsummer and the winter solstice by white robed priests. Using a golden sickle or knife the plant would fall into a cloth held by members of the order, taking care that the sacred plant did not touch the ground. Traditionally two white bulls would be sacrificed at the same time.

Sprigs of mistletoe would be distributed for the protection of homes against thunder and lightening

The plant was considered to be one of the most magical as the Celts believed that it bestowed life and fertility and that the white berries contained the sperm of the gods.

Mistletoe A native parasite on trees, found wild only in England and Wales. Height up to 3ft –1 m. Flowers February to April. Fruits November to December.

Mistletoe branches were hung from beams to ward off evil spirits, and sprigs were placed inside cribs to prevent babies from being stolen by the faeries. It was placed over doorways to prevent witches from entering the premises and mistletoe was an important addition to witch bottles; see page 149.

Decorating the house with mistletoe is an important part of the Christmas festivities; this is a remnant of the Druid traditions, but the 'kissing under the mistletoe' has its origins in the Greek festivals Saturnalia, which were held during the Yule season to celebrate the birth of Saturn.

One berry is removed with each kiss until none remains; any young girl standing underneath a bunch of mistletoe could not refuse to be kissed otherwise she would not be married in the following year. In some parts of England it is customary to burn the mistletoe on the twelfth night otherwise all the young people who had kissed beneath the mistletoe would never marry.

In Worcestershire kissing bunches were kept hanging from the beams all year until replaced by new ones. The old bunches were then burnt, a steady flame indicates a faithful husband and a spluttering flame an irritable one.

In Scandinavia the mistletoe is considered to be a plant of peace with which warring factions could declare a truce or arguing couple could use to kiss and make up. This probably has its origins in the legend of Frigga (also known as Freya), the Goddess of beauty, love and marriage. Frigga was the wife of Odin and was a sky goddess, responsible for rain and thunderstorms and as the legend goes, every time she shook out her bedding snow would fall to earth.

Frigga was also a goddess of divination; it was with this 'gift' that she foresaw the death of her son Baldur who was the God of the Summer Sun. This greatly alarmed her, for if Baldur should die then all life on earth would also perish. So in an attempt to avert this Frigga went to all things of the earth, air, fire and water, seeking a promise that they would take no part in Baldur's death but she overlooked one plant, the mistletoe.

Loki, an enemy of Baldur, discovered her mistake and fashioned a dart from the plant and took it to Baldur's brother Haldur, the blind God of Winter.

Loki suggested a game of darts and guided the blind God's hand so that he was aiming at his brother. Haldur shot the dart striking Baldur and causing his death.

The earth grew dark and all the creatures wept for the Sun God. For three days each element tried to revive the God but finally it was his mother that restored Baldur to life. Frigga's tears of joy formed into white berries on the mistletoe and in her joy at her son's recovery she still kisses everybody who passes beneath the tree on which it grows, and no harm can befall anybody who stands beneath the mistletoe.

Mistletoe was also known as 'allheal', as the berries were traditionally used to cure jaundice, whooping cough and adenoids. The plant was believed to be a cure for all childish complaints, either by wearing a garland of the berries around the neck or in a bag; but please note that the raw and unprocessed mistletoe berries are **poisonous** and can cause a drop in the heart rate, vomiting, seizure and even death. Women also used to wear the berries about their necks or arms as they believed it would help them to conceive.

Prepared berries are used to treat asthma, whooping cough, symptoms of the menopause and PM's and it is also used in cancer treatment.
It should not be used during pregnancy and while breast feeding.

The superstitions surrounding the mistletoe included the host tree; it was considered to be extremely unlucky to fell an oak that had mistletoe growing on it.
This is demonstrated by the legend that surrounds the Hay family who lived at Errol in Perthshire. The family believed that they would only prosper while their old oak, which was covered in mistletoe, continued to flourish and that it protected the family from witchcraft and stopped their babies being stolen by the faeries.
They were proved right when the oak fell in a storm and their luck changed drastically, resulting in the estate passing out of the family.

Witchbottle

A witch bottle was used to counteract any evil spells that might have been cast by witches. This practice goes back hundreds of years but was most widely used during the witch hunts; the use of the bottles declined after this period. The traditional witch bottle was made of stone and of German origin and was called a bartman or bellarmine. Named after Cardinal Robert Bellarmine, a catholic inquisitor of the 1500's. The bottle had a round belly and was decorated with a grim bearded face, presumably a portrait of the cardinal. Glass bottles were also used but were not as popular as the bellarmine style.

The bottle would contain the victim's hair (pubic and head) urine, nail clippings and bent iron nails. The bottle would then be hidden in the house, usually buried beneath the fireplace or by the front door, as it was here that the witch would be able to gain access to the building. The bottle had to remain hidden to be effective.

It was believed that the bottle would return the curse to the witch and that she would suffer agonies brought on by all the nasty things that had been placed inside the bottle.

Another method to counteract the curse was to put the bottle on the fire and allow the contents to boil while reciting the Lords prayer backwards, or the bottle could be thrown into the fire and with the bottle breaking, the curse would be lifted and the witch killed.

If the witch survived then she would have to beg the householder for the bottle to be emptied and in return for this, reverse the curse.

Witch boxes were also used in this way; they were small wooden boxes with a glass front, filled with herbs, pieces of rowan tree, paper with holy words written on it and a cross, a magic spell of protection would be cast over it. These boxes would be sold by witch hunters who traveled all over the country stirring up hysteria against witches.

Urine was also a good witch deterrent; it was sprinkled over the doorstep to prevent entry and in some cases sprinkled over people to prevent bewitchment.

Modern day witch bottles are made in much the same way only the contents vary according to the maker's beliefs. The traditional method includes menstrual blood and semen while the Wiccan witch bottle use herbs such as rosemary and mistletoe.

These modern bottles are usually used to ground negative energy and prevent harm to the home and family, although the contents can be altered to promote creativity, for financial gain, and to bring positive energy to the home.

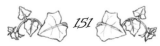

Glossary

Alkaloid......*Any series of nitrogenous basic compounds that neutralize strong acids, found in plants. Insoluble in water, Common examples are Morphine, Strychnine, Quinine, Nicotine and Coffee.*

Alimentary Canal.....*The tubular passage extending from the mouth to the anus through which food is passed and digested.*

Alzheimers.....*A common form of Dementia of unknown origin, usually beginning in late middle age, characterized by memory loss, confusion, emotional instability and loss of mental ability.*

Analgesic.....*Drug to reduce pain.*

Anti Histamine......*Certain compounds or medicines that neutralize or inhibit the effect of histamine in the body, used chiefly in the treatment of allergic disorders and colds.*

Aphrodisiac......*Producing sexual desire.*

Bronchitis.....*Inflammation of mucous membrane.*

Broths.....*Thin meat soup.*

Boron......*A mineral found in food and the environment, used for building strong bones, treating osteoarthritis, building muscles, increasing testosterone levels, improving muscular co-ordination and mental agility. Applied to skin as an astringent, prevents infection, also used as an eye wash. Used as a food preservative between 1870-1920 and during WWI and WWII.*

Catarrh....*Inflammation of a mucous membrane especially by a cold in the head.*

Carotenoids......*Any of a group of red or yellow pigments, similar to carotene, contained in animal fat and some plants.*

Chillblains.......*Itching sore on hand, foot, ear or nose due to cold.*

Colic....*Griping belly pain..*

Coma.....*Unnatural heavy sleep or stupor*

Compress....*Wet cloth applied to relieve inflammation.*

Conserve......*Fruit etc preserved in or with sugar.*

Cystitis.....*Inflammation of the urinary bladder.*

Decoction.....*Extraction of essence by boiling, liquor resulting from boiling down.*

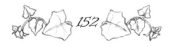

Delirium......*Disordered state of mind with incoherent speech and hallucinations.*

Dehydration......*Abnormal loss of water from the body especially from illness or physical exertion.*

Digitalis.....*A drug prepared from the dried leaves or seeds of the foxglove which is used medicinally to treat heart failure and some abnormal heart rhythms.*

Diuretic.....*Promoting secretion of urine.*

Duodenal Ulcer.....*A peptic ulcer located in the duodenum.*

Dypepsia......*Indigestion or upset stomach.*

Eczema.....*Skin disease causing inflammation of the skin.*

Embrocation......*Liquid for rubbing of limbs etc.*

Emetic.... *Causes vomiting.*

Enzyme......*Organic catalyst formed by living cells but not depending on their presence for its action.*

Estrogen.....*Main sex hormone in women and is essential to the menstrual cycle, also contributes to the fact that women have less facial hair and smoother skin than men.*

Expectorant......*Medicine promoting coughing or spitting out of phlegm from chest or lungs.*

Fibrositis.....*Inflammation of white fibrous tissue.*

Gangrene.....*Death of body tissue caused by the obstruction of the blood circulation, usually followed by decomposition and putrification.*

Gastric Ulcer......*A peptic ulcer located in the stomach's inner wall caused in part by the the corrosive action of the gastric juices on the mucous membrane.*

Germacide......*Destructive substance of germs.*

Gout.....*Disease with inflammation especially of big toe.*

Halitosis.....*Abnormally foul breath.*

Hallicinations......*Illusion of apparent perception of object not present- in mind of person.*

Hemi Parasite...... *Parasitic under natural conditions and is also photosynthetic to some degree. May just obtain water and mineral nutrients from the host plant, may also obtain part of their organic nutrients from the host plant as well.*

Hemoroids....*(Piles) swollen or twisted veins in the region of the anus and lower rectum, often painful and bleeding.*

Hydrogen Peroxide.....Unstable compound used especially as an oxidizing and bleaching agent and as an antiseptic.

Infusion.....Steeped in liquid to extract constituents.

Insomnia.... Inability to sleep.

Incontinence.....Inability to control discharge of urine or faeces.

Jaundice.... Illness due to obstruction of bile and marked by the yellowness of skin and eyes.

Laxative.....Drug to loosen the bowels.

Leucorrhoea......(otherwise known as the whites) a white or yellowish discharge of mucous material from the vagina often indicating an infection.

Lutein....(also called xanthophyll) a yellow red water insoluble crystalline carotenoid alcohol found in the petals of Marigolds and certain other flowers, egg yolks and algae.

Lye......Water alkalized with wood ashes or other alkaline solution for washing. Used for the treatment of nits.

Mange.... Skin disease caused by parasitic mites.

Neuralgia...... Sharp and paroxysmal pain along the course of a nerve.

Neuritis..... Inflammation of nerve or nerves often accompanied by pain and loss of function in the affected area.

Neuro Muscular Ailments... Very broad term that encompasses many diseases and ailments that either directly or indirectly impair the functioning of the muscles.

Paralysis.... Impairment or loss of motor or sensory functions of the nerves.

Parasite.....Animal or plant living in or on another and drawing nutriments from it.

Pectin.... Soluble gumlike carbohydrates.

Pharmacologist.....Person dealing with the preparations, uses and especially the effects of drugs.

Phospherous.....A yellowish wax-like substance oxidising in air hence appears luminous.

Philtres.....Love potion.

Plasters.....A solid or semi-solid preparation spread upon cloth or other material and applied to the body especially for healing purposes.

Poliomyelitis.....Often shortened to Polio, also called infantile

paralysis: an acute infection, viral disease, especially affecting children.

Possets.....Hot drink of milk with wine and spices as a remedy for colds etc.

Poultices.....A soft moist mass of bread, meal, herbs etc applied hot as a medicant to the body.

Propolis.....Redish resinous cement collected by bees from the buds on trees, used to stop up the holes in the hives. Also called bee glue and hive dross.

Purgative.....Medicine to purge and cleanse especially by causing evacuation of the bowels.

Reminyl.... Brand name for medication that treats Alzheimers, contains active ingredient galantamine Hydrobromide. It works by slowing the breakdown of a compound in the body called acetylcholine known as a neuro transmitter(this is used for transmitting messages between the nerve cells) One of the features of Alzheimers is a lower than normal level of acetylcholine in the brain due in part to the degeneration of brain cells, in particular the cells that release acetylcholine.

Rheumatism.....Painful disorder of joints, muscles or connective tissues.

Salve.... Healing ointment

Scabies.....Contagious skin disease caused by the itch mite which burrows under the skin.

Sciatica... See neuritis and neuralgia.

Scurvy..... Deficiency disease caused chiefly by lack of fresh vegetables and fruit.

Sinusitis...... Inflammation of sinus and sinuses.

Spleen..... Abdominal organ acting on the blood.

Styptic.... Checks bleeding-contracts the tissue or blood vessels.

Tonic.... Medicine to restore bodily tone.

Tincture... Medical solution of a drug especially in alcohol.

Urinary..... Relating to urine and its production, function or excretion.

Viscid..... Glutinous and sticky.

155

Bibliography

Aromatherapy An A to Z Patricia Davis
Vermilion 2005

Calender of Garden Lore J Jones & B Deer
Dorling Kindersley 1989

Christmas Customs & Folklore Margaret Baker
Tring 1972

Complete British Wildlife Harper Collins
Publishers Ltd 1997

Country Wisdom. Gail Duff Pan Books 1976

Culpeppers Complete Herbal Nicholas Culpepper

Curecraft Dr Keith Souter
The CW Daniel Company Ltd 1995

Curious Gardeners Almanac The. Niall Edworthy
Eden Project Books 2006

Discovering The Folklore of Plants. Margaret
Baker Shire Publications Ltd 1969

Dorset Up Along and Down Along. Womens Institute
Longmans 1935

Earth Magic. Margaret Mc Arthur
Capell Bann Publishing 1994

Enchanted World of Faeries and Elves The. Time Life
Books 1984

Encyclopedia of Witches and Witchcraft The. Rosemary
Ellen Guiley Facts on File Inc 1989

Fairies in Nineteenth Century Art & Literature Nicola
Brown Cambridge University Press 2001

Fairy Tales of Ireland WB Yeats Harper Collins
Publishing Ltd 1990

Folklore & Customs of Rural England Margaret Baker
David & Charles 1974

Folklore of Somerset The. Kingsley Palmer
B T Batsford Ltd 1976

Folktales of the British Isles The. Kevin Crossley-Holland
Faber and Faber 1985

Folklore of the Lincolnshire Marsh. Robert Heanley
The Saga Book of the Viking Club 1902
Folklore of Plants The. T F Triselton Dyer reprint of 1889
Llanerch Publishers 1994
Folklore and Symbolism of Flowers, Plants and Trees. Ernst
& Johanna Lehner Tudor Publishing Co 1960
Garden Healer The. Helen Farmer Knowles
Gaie Books 1998
Garden Spells. Claire Nahmed Pavilion Books Ltd 1994
Handbook of Folklore Charlotte Burn 1914
Herbal Magick. Gerina Dunwich New Page Books 2002
Herbs- International & Illustrated. Gilda Daisley
Cheuprime Ltd 1989
How to Grow Herbs. Ian Thomas Brockhampton Press 1999
Lincolnshire Folklore. Ethel H Rudkin Old Chapel Lane
Books 2003
Magic of Herbs The David Conway Jonathon Cape Ltd 1975
Old Wives Lore For Gardeners. Maureen & Bridget Boland
MacDonald Futura Publishers 1981
Perpetual Almanack of Folkore The. Charled Kightly
Thames & Hudson 1987
Scottish Folk & Fairy Tales. Gordon Jarvie
Penguin Books 1997
Secret Lore of Plants & Flowers The. Eric Maple
Robert Hale Ltd 1980
Traditional Remedies. Linda Gray
Ebury Press 1994
Wild Flowers of Britain. Roger Phillips Pan Books Ltd 1977
Witchcraft & Folklore of Dartmoor Ruth St Leger Gordon
Wakefield 1972

Index

I hope you enjoyed reading 'Faerie Flora' as much as I
have writing and illustrating the book.
If you did, any review you care to leave on Amazon
will help enormously!
I am always delighted to hear from readers so if you
would like to contact me please use the contact page on
my web site or alternatively find me on Facebook,
Twitter, Goodreads, Bookbub and Pinterest.
This way you will stay up to date with upcoming
books and events.
And again thanks for reading.

Elizabeth Andrews, born in the west country, has always had a great love of the countryside and its traditional folklore. She is well known for her work, specialising in the faerie world and mythical creatures and is still searching for faeries at the bottom of the garden.

For more information on Elizabeth's upcoming books and events follow the author on
Facebook
Twitter
Goodreads
Bookbub
Pinterest

Printed in Great Britain
by Amazon

79241258R00094